Oxford Revise

EDEXCEL GCSE

BUSINESS

COMPLETE REVISION AND PRACTICE

Helen Coupland-Smith
Stefan Wytwyckyj

OXFORD
UNIVERSITY PRESS

Contents

 Shade in each level of the circle as you feel more confident and ready for your exam.

How to use this book — iv

Theme 1: Investigating small business — 2–85

1 The dynamic nature of business, and risk and reward — 2
- Knowledge
- Retrieval
- Practice

2 The role of business enterprise — 8
- Knowledge
- Retrieval
- Practice

3 Customer needs — 14
- Knowledge
- Retrieval
- Practice

4 Market research — 16
- Knowledge
- Retrieval
- Practice

5 Market segmentation — 20
- Knowledge
- Retrieval
- Practice

6 The competitive environment — 24
- Knowledge
- Retrieval
- Practice

7 Business aims and objectives — 28
- Knowledge
- Retrieval
- Practice

8 Business revenues, costs and profits — 32
- Knowledge
- Retrieval
- Practice

9 Cash and cash flow — 38
- Knowledge
- Retrieval
- Practice

10 Sources of business finance — 42
- Knowledge
- Retrieval
- Practice

11 The options for start-up and small businesses	48
Knowledge	⊖
Retrieval	⊖
Practice	⊖

12 Business location	52
Knowledge	⊖
Retrieval	⊖
Practice	⊖

13 The marketing mix	56
Knowledge	⊖
Retrieval	⊖
Practice	⊖

14 Business plans	60
Knowledge	⊖
Retrieval	⊖
Practice	⊖

15 Business stakeholders	66
Knowledge	⊖
Retrieval	⊖
Practice	⊖

16 Technology and business	70
Knowledge	⊖
Retrieval	⊖
Practice	⊖

17 Legislation and business	74
Knowledge	⊖
Retrieval	⊖
Practice	⊖

18 The economy and business	78
Knowledge	⊖
Retrieval	⊖
Practice	⊖

19 External influences	82
Knowledge	⊖
Retrieval	⊖
Practice	⊖

Contents

Theme 2: Building a business — 86–169

20 Business growth — 86
- Knowledge
- Retrieval
- Practice

21 Changes in business aims and objectives — 92
- Knowledge
- Retrieval
- Practice

22 Business and globalisation — 96
- Knowledge
- Retrieval
- Practice

23 Ethics, the environment and business — 100
- Knowledge
- Retrieval
- Practice

24 Product — 106
- Knowledge
- Retrieval
- Practice

25 Price — 110
- Knowledge
- Retrieval
- Practice

26 Promotion — 112
- Knowledge
- Retrieval
- Practice

27 Place — 114
- Knowledge
- Retrieval
- Practice

28 Using the marketing mix to make business decisions — 116
- Knowledge
- Retrieval
- Practice

29 Business operations — 122
- Knowledge
- Retrieval
- Practice

30 Working with suppliers	126
⚙ Knowledge	⊖
⇄ Retrieval	⊖
✎ Practice	⊖

31 Managing quality	130
⚙ Knowledge	⊖
⇄ Retrieval	⊖
✎ Practice	⊖

32 The sales process	132
⚙ Knowledge	⊖
⇄ Retrieval	⊖
✎ Practice	⊖

33 Business calculations	136
⚙ Knowledge	⊖
⇄ Retrieval	⊖
✎ Practice	⊖

34 Understanding business performance	141
⚙ Knowledge	⊖
⇄ Retrieval	⊖
✎ Practice	⊖

35 Organisational structure	148
⚙ Knowledge	⊖
⇄ Retrieval	⊖
✎ Practice	⊖

36 Effective recruitment	154
⚙ Knowledge	⊖
⇄ Retrieval	⊖
✎ Practice	⊖

37 Effective training and development	160
⚙ Knowledge	⊖
⇄ Retrieval	⊖
✎ Practice	⊖

38 Motivation	164
⚙ Knowledge	⊖
⇄ Retrieval	⊖
✎ Practice	⊖

How to use this book

This book uses a three-step approach to revision: **Knowledge**, **Retrieval**, and **Practice**. It is important that you do all three; they work together to make your revision effective.

Knowledge

Knowledge comes first. Each chapter starts with a **Knowledge Organiser**. These are clear, easy-to-understand, concise summaries of the content that you need to know for your exam. The information is organised to show how one idea flows into the next so you can learn how everything is tied together, rather than lots of disconnected facts.

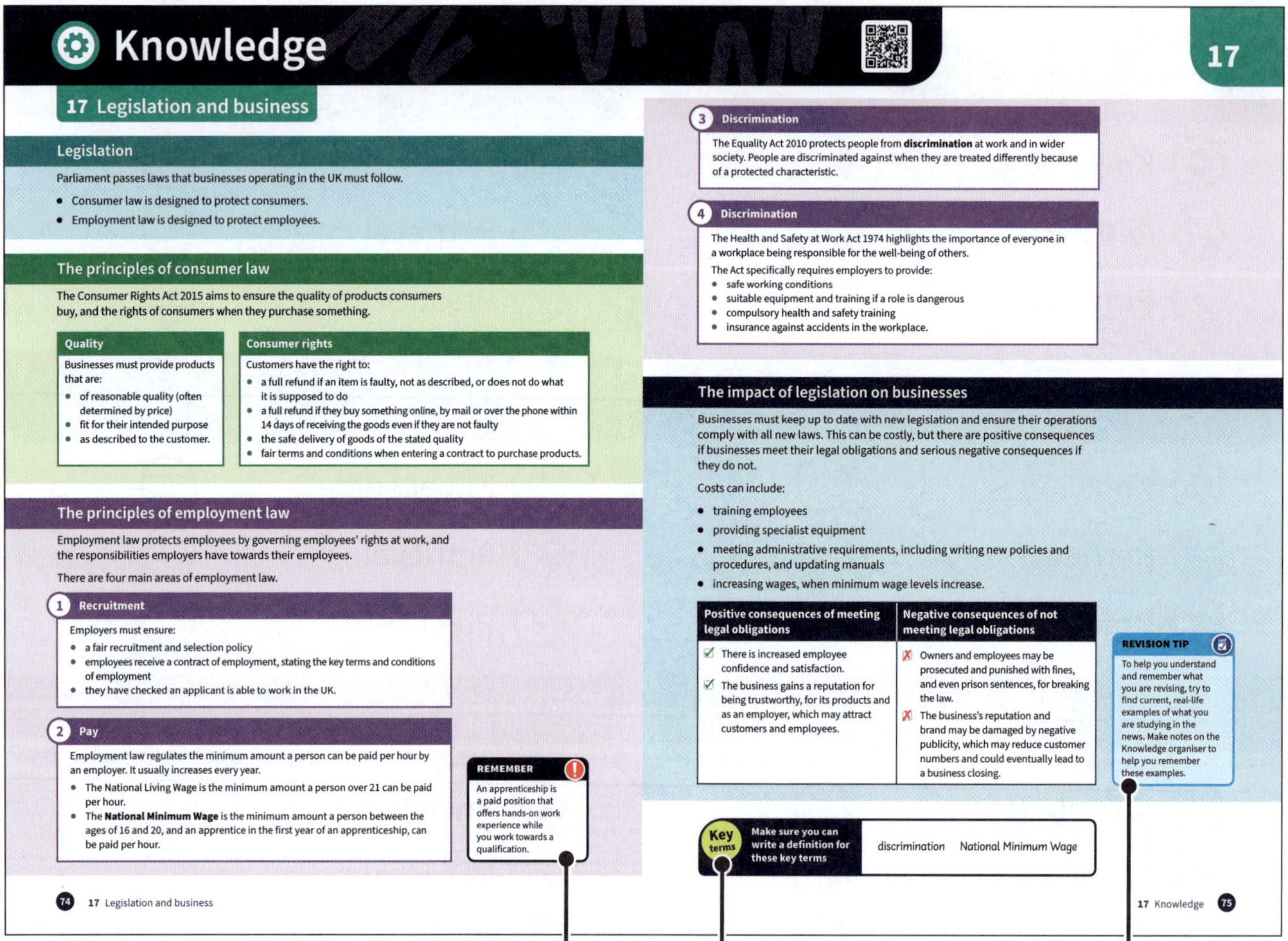

Knowledge

17

17 Legislation and business

Legislation

Parliament passes laws that businesses operating in the UK must follow.

- Consumer law is designed to protect consumers.
- Employment law is designed to protect employees.

The principles of consumer law

The Consumer Rights Act 2015 aims to ensure the quality of products consumers buy, and the rights of consumers when they purchase something.

Quality

Businesses must provide products that are:

- of reasonable quality (often determined by price)
- fit for their intended purpose
- as described to the customer.

Consumer rights

Customers have the right to:

- a full refund if an item is faulty, not as described, or does not do what it is supposed to do
- a full refund if they buy something online, by mail or over the phone within 14 days of receiving the goods even if they are not faulty
- the safe delivery of goods of the stated quality
- fair terms and conditions when entering a contract to purchase products.

The principles of employment law

Employment law protects employees by governing employees' rights at work, and the responsibilities employers have towards their employees.

There are four main areas of employment law.

1 Recruitment

Employers must ensure:

- a fair recruitment and selection policy
- employees receive a contract of employment, stating the key terms and conditions of employment
- they have checked an applicant is able to work in the UK.

2 Pay

Employment law regulates the minimum amount a person can be paid per hour by an employer. It usually increases every year.

- The National Living Wage is the minimum amount a person over 21 can be paid per hour.
- The **National Minimum Wage** is the minimum amount a person between the ages of 16 and 20, and an apprentice in the first year of an apprenticeship, can be paid per hour.

REMEMBER

An apprenticeship is a paid position that offers hands-on work experience while you work towards a qualification.

3 Discrimination

The Equality Act 2010 protects people from **discrimination** at work and in wider society. People are discriminated against when they are treated differently because of a protected characteristic.

4 Discrimination

The Health and Safety at Work Act 1974 highlights the importance of everyone in a workplace being responsible for the well-being of others.

The Act specifically requires employers to provide:

- safe working conditions
- suitable equipment and training if a role is dangerous
- compulsory health and safety training
- insurance against accidents in the workplace.

The impact of legislation on businesses

Businesses must keep up to date with new legislation and ensure their operations comply with all new laws. This can be costly, but there are positive consequences if businesses meet their legal obligations and serious negative consequences if they do not.

Costs can include:

- training employees
- providing specialist equipment
- meeting administrative requirements, including writing new policies and procedures, and updating manuals
- increasing wages, when minimum wage levels increase.

Positive consequences of meeting legal obligations	Negative consequences of not meeting legal obligations
✓ There is increased employee confidence and satisfaction. ✓ The business gains a reputation for being trustworthy, for its products and as an employer, which may attract customers and employees.	✗ Owners and employees may be prosecuted and punished with fines, and even prison sentences, for breaking the law. ✗ The business's reputation and brand may be damaged by negative publicity, which may reduce customer numbers and could eventually lead to a business closing.

REVISION TIP

To help you understand and remember what you are revising, try to find current, real-life examples of what you are studying in the news. Make notes on the Knowledge organiser to help you remember these examples.

Key terms Make sure you can write a definition for these key terms

discrimination National Minimum Wage

74 17 Legislation and business

17 Knowledge 75

Additional feature

LINK

The **Link** box appears in Theme 2 and highlights places where you should think about things you have learned in Theme 1.

REMEMBER

The **Remember** box offers useful guidance.

Key terms **Make sure you can write a definition for these key terms**

*The **Key terms** box highlights the key words and phrases you need to know, remember, and be able to use confidently.*

REVISION TIP

Revision tips offer you helpful advice and guidance to aid your revision and help you to understand key concepts and remember them.

Retrieval

The **Retrieval questions** help you learn and quickly recall the information you've acquired. These are short questions and answers about the content in the Knowledge Organiser you have just reviewed. Cover up the answers with some paper and write down as many answers as you can from memory. Check back to the Knowledge Organiser for any you got wrong, then cover the answers and attempt all the questions again until you can answer *all* the questions correctly.

Make sure you revisit the Retrieval questions on different days to help them stick in your memory. You need to write down the answers each time, or say them out loud, otherwise it won't work.

Previous questions

Each chapter also has some **Retrieval questions** from **previous chapters**. Answer these to see if you can remember the content from the earlier chapters. If you get the answers wrong, go back and do the Retrieval questions for the earlier chapters again.

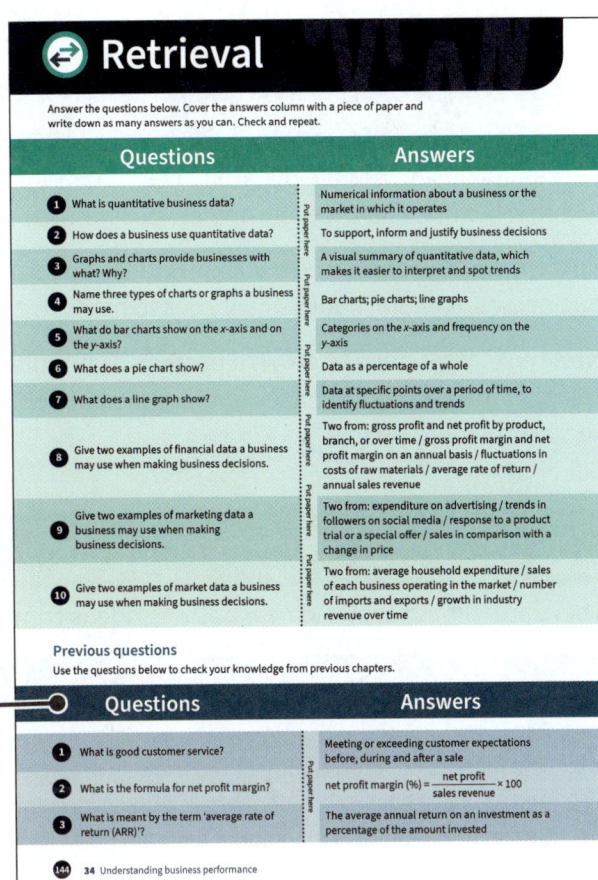

Practice

Once you are confident with the Knowledge Organisers and Retrieval questions, you can move on to the final stage: **Practice**.

Each chapter has **exam-style questions** to help you apply all the knowledge you have learned.

EXAM TIP

Exam tips show you how to interpret the questions, provide guidance on how to answer them, and give advice on how to secure as many marks as possible.

Answers and Glossary

You can scan the QR code at any time to access sample answers and mark schemes for all the exam-style questions, a glossary containing definitions of the key terms, as well as further revision support.
Visit go.oup.com/OR/GCSE/Ed/Bus

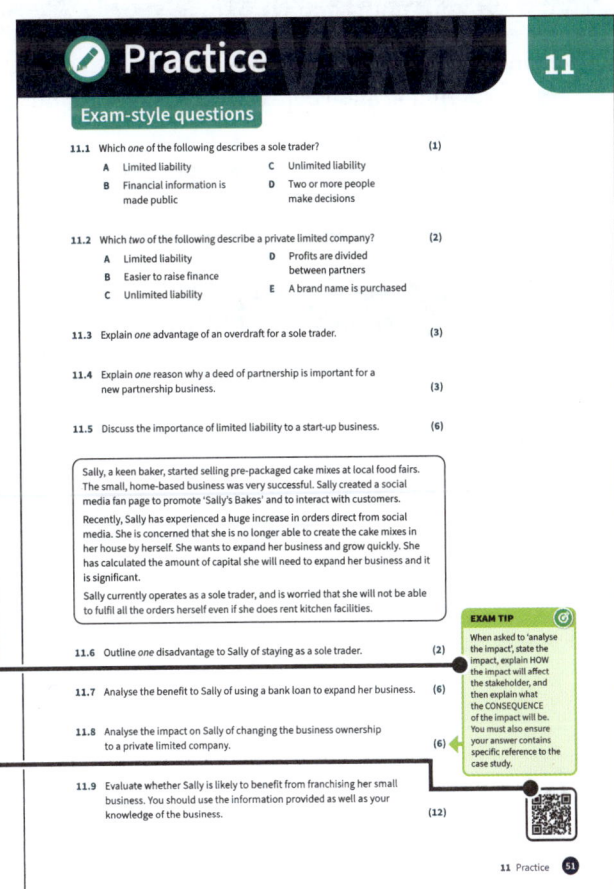

 Knowledge

1 The dynamic nature of business, and risk and reward

The importance of new business ideas

Successful businesses are dynamic. They change in response to internal and external factors, and they rely on new business ideas to evolve and stay relevant.

Entrepreneurs identify new business ideas and use these ideas to start new businesses, creating goods or services to meet customer needs.

New businesses need to grow to become profitable. Business growth relies on selling more goods or services to the same people, or selling more goods or services to more people.

> **REMEMBER**
> Internal factors, such as working hours and salaries, are within a business's control. External factors, such as **legislation** and the economy, are outside a business's control.

Why new business ideas come about

There are three main ways new business ideas come about.

Changes in technology

- Rapid technological changes mean completely new business ideas can be created.
- The increasing affordability of technology means more customers can buy goods and services based on technology that was previously unaffordable.
- **Social media** allows for quicker and more efficient communication, helping large and small businesses market new goods and services to wider audiences.

Changes in what customers want

- Changes in customers' lifestyles impact the popularity of goods and services.
- Better communication between customers and businesses means customer needs can be more easily identified.
- **Data tracking** helps businesses to design and redesign products to meet changing customer needs.

Obsolescence

- Products become **obsolete** if they are not adapted.
- Technologies become out of date and need replacing or updating.
- Habits, tastes and fashions change, and goods and services need to change with them.

How new business ideas come about

Businesses have a choice between coming up with original ideas for new goods or services, or adapting existing goods or services.

Original ideas

Coming up with original ideas for new goods and services is very difficult: you have to be both **creative** and have **insight** into what customers want. Original ideas can come through **invention** or **innovation**.

Invention

- Can a new **product** improve something that already exists?
- How can this something be improved?
- Is there something I want or something I want to do that does not yet exist?

Innovation

- Can I solve a problem with an existing product?
- How do I improve a product to solve the problem?

Adaptation

There are many ways a product can be altered to sell better.

Adaptation

- Changing the name of a **brand** to keep it up to date, to respond to cultural changes, or to sell it in new markets.
- Creating specific versions of a product to meet specific customer needs.
- Changing the format of a product by altering the colour, size or shape to better meet customer needs, to respond to changing fashions, to incorporate new technology, or to respond to a change in the law.
- Changing **promotional strategies** to respond to changing media trends, or adapting the pricing model.

Adaptation is less of a **risk** than launching a brand-new product: potential customers may already be familiar with the product, making them more likely to buy it. However, there is still risk involved:

- Is the customer base large enough to justify the **investment**?
- Will the adapted product meet customer needs, or will customers turn to another business for what they want?

> **REVISION TIP**
>
> Most people can concentrate best for short periods of time, so remember to take breaks during your revision.

Knowledge

1 The dynamic nature of business, and risk and reward

Risk and reward

Entrepreneurs take risks when setting up new businesses. However, if the new business is successful, then the entrepreneur will gain **rewards** for their hard work.

Risk

Business failure
Poor planning and decision-making, often arising from poor **market research**, can lead to **cash flow** problems. Lower than expected **sales revenue** can occur because of an economic downturn, strong competition, or a non-viable business idea.

Financial loss
The financial investment an entrepreneur makes into a **start-up** can be lost if the business fails or is not as successful as expected.

Lack of security
Not all new businesses are successful, and many new businesses take a while to make a **profit**. As a result, many entrepreneurs experience a lack of financial stability. Entrepreneurs often invest lots of time and effort into their new business, which can be stressful and have a negative impact on their health and well-being.

Reward

Business success
The new business meets, and possibly exceeds, the expectations of the entrepreneur and their investors. This could mean achieving **sales targets** or receiving industry awards.

Profit
The new business makes a profit. Most entrepreneurs would like the profits from their business to be higher than the income they could make working for another business.

Independence
Some entrepreneurs gain satisfaction from the independence of being their own boss, running a successful company, and increasing their personal wealth.

Maximising success by minimising risks

Successful entrepreneurs try to maximise their chances of success by minimising the level of risk they incur. They use market research and revenue forecasts to do this.

Market research

They gather information from the market and use it to support decision-making.

Information gathered includes customer needs and wants, the **strengths** and **weaknesses** of competing products and the proposed product, and sales and marketing ideas.

Revenue forecasts

They predict future **revenue** based on **revenue forecasts**.

These **forecasts** can be based on judgment, market research, and previous sales data.

 Key terms — Make sure you can write a definition for these key terms

adaptation   brand   cash flow   creative   data tracking
entrepreneur   forecast   innovation   insight   invention
investment   legislation   market research   obsolete   product
profit   promotional strategy   revenue   revenue forecast
reward   risk   sales revenue   sales target   social media
start-up   strength   weakness

> **REVISION TIP**
>
> Create flow charts to help you visualise how key terms link together. You can make brief annotations to show connections.

1 Knowledge

Retrieval

Answer the questions below. Cover the answers column with a piece of paper and write down as many answers as you can. Check and repeat.

Questions / Answers

1. What do new businesses rely on to evolve and stay relevant?
— New business ideas

2. List the three main ways new business ideas come about.
— Changes in technology; changes in what customers want; obsolescence

3. Give one way changes in technology can lead to new business ideas.
— One from: rapid technological changes mean completely new business ideas can be created / the increasing affordability of technology means more customers can buy goods and services based on technology that was previously unaffordable / social media allows for quicker and more efficient communication, helping large and small businesses market new goods and services to wider audiences

4. Give one way changes in what customers want can lead to new business ideas.
— One from: changes in customers' lifestyles impact the popularity of goods and services / better communication between customers and businesses means that customer needs can be more easily identified / data tracking helps businesses to design and redesign products to meet changing customer needs

5. There are two ways to come up with new business ideas. What are they?
— Coming up with original ideas for new goods or services; adapting existing goods or services

6. How do entrepreneurs come up with original ideas?
— Through invention or innovation

7. List four ways a product can be adapted to sell better.
— Changing the name of a brand; changing the format of a product; creating specific versions to meet specific customer needs; changing promotional strategies

8. Why is adapting a product less of a risk than launching a brand-new product?
— Potential customers may already be familiar with the product, making them more likely to buy it

9. What are the three main risks of setting up a new business?
— Business failure; financial loss; lack of security

10. What does business success look like?
— Meeting, and possibly exceeding, the expectations of the entrepreneur and their investors

11. List two types of information gathered during market research.
— Two from: customer needs and wants / the strengths and weaknesses of competing products and the proposed product / sales and marketing ideas

12. What do entrepreneurs use to minimise the level of risk they incur and maximise their chances of success?
— Market research and revenue forecasts

1 The dynamic nature of business, and risk and reward

Practice 1

Exam-style questions

1.1 Which *one* of the following is a reward of entrepreneurial activity? (1)
- A Business failure
- B Independence
- C Financial loss
- D Lack of security

> **EXAM TIP**
> Before attempting to answer each question, use the 'BUG' method:
> - Box the command word so that you know what you are being asked to do.
> - Underline the key words (the words that tell you which topic the question is about, and jog your memory about the topic).
> - Glance at the question again to pick up any additional information it is giving you and to help you picture what you need to do.

1.2 Which *two* of the following are ways new business ideas come about? (2)
- A Changes in technology
- B Selling more products
- C Finding more customers
- D Obsolescence
- E Business growth

1.3 Explain *one* risk associated with starting a new business. (3)

1.4 Explain *one* way in which an entrepreneur can minimise their level of risk when setting up a new business. (3)

1.5 Discuss how decision-making in a new business may be affected by an entrepreneur's willingness to take risks. (6)

> **EXAM TIP**
> One approach to a 'Discuss' question is to write a relevant point plus three strands, followed by a second relevant point plus two strands. A strand is a development point. Try using connectives – 'this means that', 'leading to', 'therefore' – to join your strands.

John Smith works as a bicycle engineer for ABC Bikes Ltd, a small independent bicycle shop, which focuses on selling and servicing pedal cycles within a limited geographical area. Many customers are enquiring about electric bicycles, but the owner of ABC Bikes Ltd does not want to invest in expensive e-bikes or the equipment needed to service them.

John is an entrepreneur and has recently been paying for someone to teach him how to service e-bikes, because he thinks there is an opportunity to set up his own e-bike sales and servicing business.

1.6 Define the term 'entrepreneur'. (1)

1.7 State *one* reason why John Smith's business idea has come about. (1)

1.8 Outline *one* reason why market research could be important to ABC Bikes Ltd. (2)

1.9 Analyse the risks John Smith will be taking if he sets up an e-bike sales and servicing business. (6)

Knowledge

2 The role of business enterprise

The role of business enterprise

Business enterprise is the setting up, or the expansion, of a business by an entrepreneur or another business.

The main role of business enterprise is often considered to be making as much profit as possible. However, it can have other roles depending on who the **stakeholder** is. A stakeholder is anyone who has an interest in, or is affected by, the activities of a business.

Owners
- Meet customer **needs**
- Maximise growth
- Maximise profit

The role of business enterprise by stakeholder

Local community
- Meet social responsibilities
- Act **ethically**

Employees
- Provide employment
- Pay the **National Living Wage**

Customers
- Provide goods or services

Government
- Create jobs
- Create **economic growth**
- Increase living standards across the country

The purpose of business activity

Business activity has three main purposes.

1. To produce goods or services
Businesses must produce goods and services that customers want to buy. If goods and services are sold, the profit can be reinvested, which leads to further business growth.

2. To meet customer needs
Goods and services are successful when they meet customers' needs, and businesses understand their customers' needs by carrying out market research and by building relationships with customers.

Customer needs include a range of factors such as quick delivery times, competitive prices, enough **stock** available in store or online, and well-thought-out websites.

3. To add value
Businesses want to **add value** to their goods and services to maximise profit. Common ways of adding value include:

REMEMBER

Identify different customer needs before deciding which methods of adding value are important. Not all customers want the same thing, and what can add value for one group of customers may not be important for another group.

Convenience
Making a product easy to buy is key to adding value. Opening times (for physical shops), great **customer service**, a variety of payment methods, and lots of stock are important for attracting customers and ensuring they want to return.

Branding
Value can be added by creating a brand. A brand is a distinct identity. It consists of a name, a logo, slogans, the defining **values** of a product, and how they are communicated to customers. The **aim** is to create customers who are loyal to a brand and choose it over competitor brands.

Quality

A product must meet customer expectations and customers must be able to depend upon it to do its job. If customers trust the **quality**, they are more likely to buy an expensive product than a cheaper version of unknown quality.

Design

The look and feel of not only the product, but also the marketing and the shop or website where it is purchased can add value. An innovative design is more likely to gain customer attention, even if the product is the same as a competitor product.

Unique selling point

A **unique selling point** is a noticeable point of difference between your product and a competitor's product to attract customers. A USP can be based on price, quality, or being first to **market**.

The role of entrepreneurship

Entrepreneurship is vital to a country's **economy** and, therefore, to society as a whole. If people are not willing to start new businesses, there may be a lack of jobs and the economy could decline.

In addition to having a new business idea, entrepreneurs must make their new businesses a success, by organising resources, making business decisions and taking risks.

Organising resources

Resources include land, labour and capital (the finance used to start and maintain a business), as well as materials.

An entrepreneur must have somewhere to conduct their business activities, must have enough employees, and must have the skills to motivate, lead and manage their employees, as well as enough finance to cover all costs in the short term and the long term.

Making business decisions

Entrepreneurs must make important business decisions, such as who to employ, how much finance to spend on developing their new business idea, and how much their customers should be charged for the product they are selling.

Business decisions must consider both **short-term** requirements and the **long-term** vision, and focus on meeting customer needs and making a profit.

Taking risks

It is impossible to avoid taking risks when developing a new business idea. However, an entrepreneur must assess the level of risk they are comfortable taking and act accordingly.

Risks can be both financial (such as how much to spend) and operational (such as the time given to developing the new product).

Risks can be minimised with good market knowledge gained through effective market research.

Key terms — Make sure you can write a definition for these key terms

add value   aim   business enterprise   customer service   economic growth   economy   ethically   long-term   market   National Living Wage   need   quality   short-term   stakeholder   stock   unique selling point (USP)   value

Retrieval

Answer the questions below. Cover the answers column with a piece of paper and write down as many answers as you can. Check and repeat.

Questions and Answers

#	Questions	Answers
1	What is business enterprise?	The setting up, or the expansion, of a business by an entrepreneur or another business
2	What is the main role of business enterprise often considered to be?	Make as much profit as possible
3	As well as maximising profit, what other roles does business enterprise have for business owners?	Meeting customer needs; maximising growth
4	What three roles does business enterprise have for government?	Creating jobs; creating economic growth; increasing living standards across the country
5	State the three main purposes of business activity.	To produce goods or services; to meet customer needs; to add value
6	Customer needs include a range of factors. Give three factors.	Three from: quick delivery times / competitive prices / enough stock available in store or online / well-thought-out websites or something similar
7	Give five ways businesses can add value to their goods and services.	Convenience; branding; quality; design; unique selling point (USP)
8	What does a brand consist of?	A name, a logo, slogans, the defining values of a business, and how they are communicated to customers
9	What is a unique selling point (USP)?	A noticeable point of difference between your product and a competitor's product to attract customers
10	Why is entrepreneurship vital to a country's economy?	If people are not willing to start new businesses, there may be a lack of jobs and the economy could decline
11	What are the three roles of entrepreneurship?	Organising resources; making business decisions; taking risks

Previous questions

Use the questions below to check your knowledge from previous chapters.

#	Questions	Answers
1	List the three main ways new business ideas come about.	Changes in technology; changes in what customers want; obsolescence
2	List four ways a product or service can be adapted to sell better.	Changing the name of a brand; changing the format of a product; creating specific versions to meet specific customer needs; changing promotional strategies
3	What are the three main risks of setting up a new business?	Business failure; financial loss; lack of security

Practice 2

Exam-style questions

2.1 Which *one* of the following is a way to add value to a product? **(1)**
  A Build in obsolescence
  B Develop a USP
  C Reduce cost of sales
  D Paying employees the National Living Wage

2.2 Which *two* of the following are not aspects of branding? **(2)**
  A Slogan
  B Logo
  C Payment methods
  D Design
  E Private limited company

2.3 Explain *one* way in which an entrepreneur can add value to a product. **(3)**

2.4 Explain *one* reason why an entrepreneur must organise resources effectively. **(3)**

2.5 Discuss the importance to an entrepreneur of balancing risk and reward. **(6)**

> Village Stores Ltd is a community shop in a small village. It sells magazines, fresh and frozen locally-produced food, and has a small self-service coffee machine.
>
> Many cyclists stop at Village Stores Ltd and buy a cold drink or a snack. The employees have overheard the cyclists saying they are unhappy with the coffee facilities, and lack of a seating area, something many local customers also complain of.

EXAM TIP
Briefly planning answers to higher-mark questions will help you structure your answer well, reducing the chances of repetition and increasing the chances of applying relevant knowledge or examples.

2.6 State *one* role of business enterprise that is not being achieved by Village Stores Ltd. **(1)**

EXAM TIP
Read each question carefully and ensure the amount you write reflects the number of marks available. Do not, for example, write half a page in answer to a 1-mark question.

2.7 Outline *one* way in which Village Stores Ltd would add value if the coffee facilities were upgraded and a seating area was provided. **(2)**

2.8 Outline *one* benefit to Village Stores Ltd of reorganising in response to customer feedback. **(2)**

2.9 Analyse the risks that Village Stores Ltd could face if the coffee facilities were upgraded and a seating area was provided. **(6)**

Practice

Exam-style questions

Banger Bytes is an electric car designed and produced by Banger Cars. The business was formed in 2017 by Lord Bob Hope. He came up with the idea because he saw the growing popularity of electric cars, and the economic incentives being provided for car manufacturers to encourage them to meet environmental targets.

Banger Cars was formed with the aim of making electric cars affordable. It entered into a partnership with Oldcar, a struggling petrol and diesel car manufacturer, which provided the body of the vehicle. Batteries and electronics were sourced from low-cost international suppliers. The car was designed to meet minimum safety requirements, and was priced lower than existing competition. Instead of using traditional and expensive car showrooms, Banger Cars relies on social media to market and sell its cars.

In the last four years, imports of technologically superior electric cars have been reducing Banger Cars' market share. The Banger Cars brand is a low-cost brand, and this is no longer the advantage it once was as customers seek more advanced technology. Banger Cars has been designing a new car that better meets customers' needs. However, an opportunity has arisen to partner with ElecCars, a reputable electric car brand that wants to enter the British market.

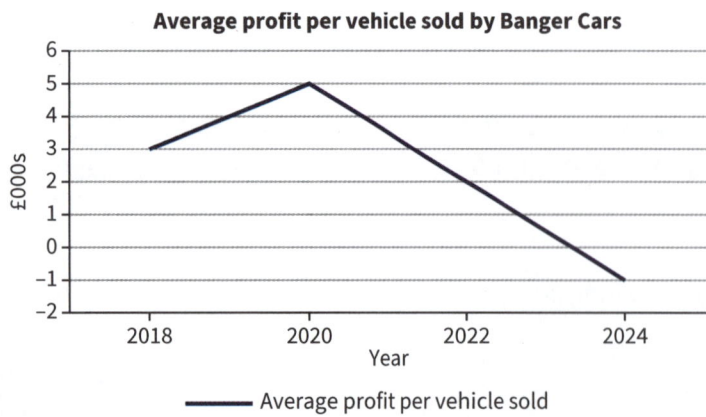

▲ **Figure 1** Banger Cars' average profit per car sold

2.10 State *one* way Banger Cars could identify customer needs. **(1)**

2.11 Give *one* example of how Banger Cars adapted an existing product. **(1)**

2.12 Using the information in Figure 1, identify the year when Banger Cars made a loss. **(1)**

2.13 Outline *one* risk taken by Lord Bob Hope when starting Banger Cars. **(2)**

2.14 Outline *one* USP of Banger Cars. **(2)**

2.15 Analyse the impact on Banger Cars of using social media to sell their products. **(6)**

> **EXAM TIP**
>
> When marking 'Justify' questions, the examiner is looking for balance. This means that you must present both sides of the argument. For example, if you choose Option 2, you should write one paragraph about the advantage of Option 2 and a second paragraph about the disadvantage of Option 2.

2.16 Banger Cars' products have become obsolete. It is now considering two options:

Option 1: remain independent

Option 2: partner with ElecCars.

Justify which one of these two options Banger Cars should choose. **(9)**

> **EXAM TIP**
>
> To fully answer Question 2.17, you might want to look ahead to Chapter 16 and revise the different types of technology used by business, and how technology influences business activity. Or you could come back to this question when you've revised Chapter 16.

2.17 Evaluate the impact of changes in technology on Banger Cars' business. You should use the information provided as well as your knowledge of business. **(12)**

Knowledge

3 Customer needs

Identifying and understanding customer needs

There are two ways to identify customer needs:

- Personal experience: many people are able to spot what is wrong with, or missing from, a product they want. When this happens, their needs as a customer are unfulfilled. Most people will buy the product that is closest to their needs. An entrepreneur will try to create a product to meet these unfulfilled needs.
- Spotting an opportunity: entrepreneurs are able to meet needs that have previously been impossible to meet, or meet needs that nobody has identified as needs. Changes in technology have created a lot of opportunities like this.

There are four main customer needs that must be satisfied:

Price

Businesses consider factors such as the cost of production, competitors' prices, business aims and **objectives**, and the state of the economy to make a final decision on how much to charge customers.

Prices can either be high, if there is high customer demand or a business wants to create a sense of exclusivity (**premium pricing**), or low, to attract the maximum number of customers (**loss leaders**).

Quality

Quality depends on the expectations of the customer. A 'quality' product must be fit for purpose and complete the task required for the right price.

Quality is not just linked to high prices: low-priced disposable products that fulfil the expectations of a customer can be considered 'high quality'.

Choice

Different customers have different tastes and needs, based on different cultural, societal, or individual requirements, such as price and quality.

Customers wanting choice leads to **product differentiation**, which makes it easier for a customer to choose the most appropriate product from the selection offered by a business.

Convenience

For physical stores, convenience can include location, opening hours, and delivery options. For online businesses, convenience can include delivery options, and different payment options.

Customers are more likely to shop at businesses that make it as easy as possible to access the products available, and may pay a higher price for greater convenience.

The importance of identifying and understanding customer needs

Identifying and understanding customer needs is essential for generating sales and for business survival.

Generating sales is important for all businesses. If a business does not have any customers, then it cannot make any sales. If there are no sales, there will be no profit. If there is no profit, the business will fail. → Business survival is essential. If a business has poor cash flow, it will not be able to pay its bills, including rent, **wages** and **salaries**. High sales with low profits can cause cash flow issues.

Key terms — Make sure you can write a definition for these key terms: loss leader, objective, premium pricing, product differentiation, salary, wage

Retrieval 3

Answer the questions below. Cover the answers column with a piece of paper and write down as many answers as you can. Check and repeat.

Questions | Answers

#	Question	Answer
1	State two ways to identify customer needs.	Personal experience; spotting an opportunity
2	What are the four customer needs that must be satisfied?	Price; quality; choice; convenience
3	Customers have different tastes and needs. Why?	Because they have different cultural, societal or individual requirements
4	Why is it important to identify and understand customer needs?	To generate sales and ensure business survival

Put paper here

Previous questions

Use the questions below to check your knowledge from previous chapters.

Questions | Answers

#	Question	Answer
1	What three roles does business enterprise have for government?	Creating jobs; creating economic growth; increased living standards across the country
2	Customer needs include a range of factors. Give three factors.	Three from: quick delivery times / competitive prices / enough stock available in store or online / well-thought-out websites or something similar

Put paper here

Practice

Exam-style questions

3.1 Which *two* of the following elements of convenience are relevant to online businesses? (2)

    A Opening hours   **D** Payment options

    B Delivery options   **E** Location

    C Parking

3.2 Explain *one* reason why the quality of a business's products is important for its survival. (3)

3.3 Discuss the impact of changes in technology on a business. (6)

> **EXAM TIP**
>
> You may not know the correct answer to a multiple-choice question, but you may be able to identify one or more incorrect answers. This will help you narrow down your remaining choices.

3 Retrieval 15

Knowledge

4 Market research

What is market research?

Market research is the process of collecting and analysing information about three key areas:

1 Market
- Current and future market trends
- The size of the market
- The expected selling price

2 Competitors
- Who the biggest competitors are
- How large their market share is
- What the strengths and weaknesses of their products are

3 Customers
- Current customer needs and wants
- Factors that influence buying decisions
- Where and how customers purchase products

The purpose of market research

Market research helps businesses to:

1. identify and understand customer needs
2. identify gaps in the market
3. reduce risk
4. inform business decisions.

For example, a business can use market research to test the market to see whether a business idea is likely to be successful, or to find out what improvements are needed to current products.

Methods of market research

There are two main methods of market research.

Primary research collects first-hand (original) data, which did not previously exist and is specific to the current problem.

Secondary research reviews existing data, which has already been collected for another purpose, either within the business or outside the business.

1 Types of primary research

- **Surveys**: a survey uses one or more different types of primary research to answer research questions. A survey can include a questionnaire, but it can also include focus groups, interviews and observations.
- **Questionnaires**: a questionnaire is a series of questions. Questionnaires can contain both **open questions** and **closed questions,** but usually contain closed questions to gather **quantitative data**. Questionnaires can be administered face to face or online; online questionnaires usually gather more responses than face-to-face questionnaires.
- **Interviews**: an interview is an in-depth one-to-one conversation. Interviews can contain both open and closed questions, but usually contain open questions to gather **qualitative data**. Interviews can take place face to face, online or over the telephone.
- **Focus groups**: a focus group is a facilitated group discussion. The facilitator asks a **sample** of the **target market** a series of questions, encouraging open discussion to gain a deeper understanding of customers' opinions. Focus groups often last over an hour, and can take place face to face or online.
- **Observations**: researchers watch how customers behave in a natural setting, and record what they see. Observations can provide useful information about how customers move around a shop, for example. However, observations on their own cannot explain why customers do what they do.

2 Types of secondary research

- **Internal research:** businesses collect many types of data for specific reasons. If the data are later used for another reason, then it is classed as secondary research.
- **External research:** important insights, particularly about the wider market, can be gained from information published by organisations and people not related to a business. For example, government departments, such as the Office for National Statistics, trade associations and universities publish data and reports that can help businesses make decisions. This sort of information is now easily available online.

> **REVISION TIP**
>
> It is important to know the difference between closed questions and open questions.
> - Closed questions are questions where the responses are limited to a set number of pre-determined options. Open questions are unlimited, allowing the respondent to answer in their own way.
> - Closed questions generate quantitative data: numerical data that are easy to collect, count and analyse. Open questions generate qualitative data: non-numerical (descriptive) data that are harder to analyse but help us understand things such as behaviours and feelings.

> **REMEMBER**
>
> The target market is everyone the research wants to study, while the sample is a smaller group of people that stand in for the target market.

The role of social media in collecting market research data

Social media is a cheap and efficient way to collect both primary and secondary data, and qualitative and quantitative data about customers and the market.

- It is an easy way to contact and talk with customers to identify trends.
- It helps businesses develop products and market them because they can join in discussions rather than just ask questions.
- It provides an up-to-date view of the target market and what competitors are doing.
- It saves time because data can be collected and analysed continuously using technology, and can be collected from a large sample size.

The importance of the reliability of market research data

In order to be reliable, data needs to have a high level of **validity** and be **representative** of the target market.

High level of validity

Market research with a high level of validity accurately represents the target market.

For example, questionnaires with a narrow range of questions that push the respondent towards specific answers do not have a high level of validity.

Representative

If the data is gathered from an accurate sample of the target market, it is representative.

For example, if the target market is all 14- to 16-year-olds in the UK, a representative sample will include 14- to 16-year-olds from across the country. It will not include 13-year-olds or 17-year-olds, and it will not focus exclusively on young people living in cities.

Key terms — Make sure you can write a definition for these key terms:

closed question focus group interview observation open question primary research qualitative data quantitative data questionnaire representative sample secondary research survey target market validity

4 Knowledge

Retrieval

Answer the questions below. Cover the answers column with a piece of paper and write down as many answers as you can. Check and repeat.

	Questions	Answers
1	Market research is the process of collecting and analysing information from what three key areas?	Market; competitors; customers
2	State two purposes of market research.	Two from: to help businesses identify and understand customer needs / to help businesses identify gaps in the market / to help businesses reduce risk / to inform business decisions
3	There are two main methods of market research. What are they?	Primary research; secondary research
4	Give two types of primary research.	Two from: surveys / questionnaires / interviews / focus groups / observations
5	What is the difference between closed questions and open questions?	Closed questions are questions where the responses are limited to a set number of pre-determined options. Open questions are unlimited, allowing the respondent to answer in their own way
6	What is the difference between quantitative data and qualitative data?	Quantitative data are numerical data that are easy to collect, count and analyse. Qualitative data are non-numerical (descriptive) data that are harder to analyse but help us understand things such as behaviours and feelings
7	Give two types of secondary research.	Internal research; external research
8	List three sources of external research.	Government departments; trade associations; universities
9	How do you ensure market research data is reliable?	It needs to have a high level of validity and be representative of the target market

Previous questions

Use the questions below to check your knowledge from previous chapters.

	Questions	Answers
1	State the three main purposes of business activity.	To produce goods or services; to meet customer needs; to add value
2	What are the four customer needs that must be satisfied?	Price; quality; choice; convenience
3	Why is it important to identify and understand customer needs?	To generate sales and ensure business survival

4 Market research

Practice

4

Exam-style questions

4.1 Which *one* of the following is a key area of interest for market research? **(1)**

  A Proximity to materials
  B Cash flow
  C Competitors
  D Sources of short-term finance

4.2 Which *two* of the following are types of secondary research? **(2)**

  A Questionnaires
  B Observations
  C Report on the state of the market
  D Focus groups
  E Data from the Office of National Statistics

4.3 Explain *one* way in which secondary research can help in decision-making. **(3)**

4.4 Discuss the value of qualitative data when carrying out market research. **(6)**

> Dingo's Diner is a chain of fast-food restaurants specialising in gourmet burgers. It has had vegetarian burgers on its menu for a long time due to customer demand.
>
> John, the owner, has recently been wondering whether it is worth selling vegan burgers to increase the choice available to customers. He is concerned that, while vegan burgers are trending on social media, very few customers have enquired about vegan options.

EXAM TIP

When answering case study questions, you are required to apply the information in the case study to the questions. This means you must refer to the case study in your answers. Use a highlighter to highlight useful information in the case study to help you do this.

4.5 Define the term 'choice'. **(1)**

4.6 State *one* primary research method other than observation that John could use to estimate demand for vegan burgers. **(1)**

4.7 Outline *one* way in which John could ensure the validity of his research into the demand for vegan burgers. **(2)**

4.8 John has been presented with two options for market research:

  Option 1: internet research to find out more about the market for vegan food

  Option 2: questionnaires for his customers.

  Justify which *one* of these two options John should choose. **(9)**

Knowledge

5 Market segmentation

Using market segmentation to target customers

Breaking the **mass market**, the whole market, down into smaller parts is known as **market segmentation**. Market segmentation helps businesses develop specific goods and services to meet the needs of specific groups of customers.

There are three elements to market segmentation:

Identify specific customer requirements → **Create distinct market segments** → **Market specific products to each market segment**

- By understanding common needs or interests, it is possible to identify specific customer requirements.
- Customers who share similar characteristics can be grouped into categories.
- Goods and services that meet the specific needs of each market segment can be marketed directly to target customers to maximise sales.

Identifying market segments

Market segments can be identified using market research to group customers by a series of categories.

> **REVISION TIP**
>
> When revising market segmentation, choose a product that you like and describe the market segment it is aimed at. Then make a market map: choose two features for the axes and plot the product you like and its competitors.

Categories: Location, Demographics, Lifestyle, Income, Age

↓

Market segment: for example, women with high disposable incomes, aged 19–29, who live in cities and visit the gym regularly

Location

Geographical segmentation groups people into locations, usually where they live.
- People living in rural areas will often have different needs to people living in cities, who may also have different needs to people living in towns.
- Knowing the type of home a person lives in (e.g. whether they live in a flat or a house) can help a business predict their buying behaviour, including the products and brands they will buy.

5 Market segmentation

Demographics

Demographic segmentation groups people by social and economic characteristics, including age, stage in life, gender, level of education, religion, family size, and income.

Lifestyle

People can be grouped by how they choose to live their lives, including their activities, interests and opinions.

Segmenting by lifestyle can help a business customise its marketing to increase its relevance.

Customers of lifestyle goods and services are more likely to be loyal to a brand if the brand's image fits with their own self-image.

Age

As customers age, their needs change. What is suitable for one age group may not be suitable for another age group.

Style and fashion may be more attractive to younger customers, while practicality and price may be more important for older customers.

Income

The amount of money people earn affects their **disposable income** (how much money they have left after paying for essentials), which, in turn, influences what they can afford to buy.

Goods and services with a higher added value attract richer customers, and they should be advertised in places where richer customers are most likely to see them.

Market mapping

Market mapping helps businesses identify gaps in the market.

A market map plots competitors' products on two axes. If there is a space on the map, this may indicate an unmet demand.

Features often used to label market map axes include price, quality, ease of use, and level of innovation.

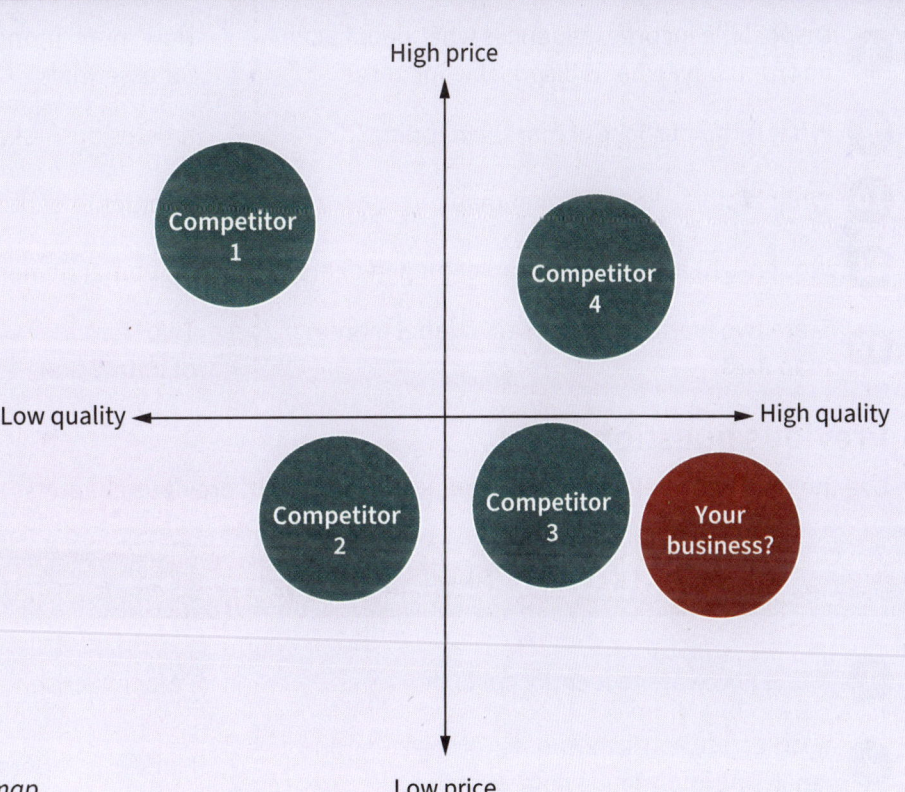

▶ Figure 1 *An example of a market map*

Key terms — Make sure you can write a definition for these key terms

disposable income   market segmentation   mass market

Retrieval

Answer the questions below. Cover the answers column with a piece of paper and write down as many answers as you can. Check and repeat.

Questions / Answers

#	Question	Answer
1	What is market segmentation?	Breaking the mass market down into smaller parts
2	What are the three elements of market segmentation?	Identify specific customer requirements; create distinct market segments; market specific products to each market segment
3	How can market segments be identified?	Using market research
4	Identify two categories used to segment the market.	Two from: location / demographics / lifestyle / income / age
5	State two ways in which demographics groups people.	Two from: age / stage of life / gender / level of education / religion / family size / income
6	Give two aspects of lifestyles that can be used to group people.	Two from: activities / interests / opinions
7	When are customers of lifestyle goods and services more likely to be loyal to a brand?	When the brand's image fits with their own self-image
8	Disposable income influences what people can afford to buy. What is disposable income?	How much money you have left after paying for essentials
9	What is the purpose of market mapping?	It helps businesses identify gaps in the market
10	What is plotted on a market map?	Competitors' products
11	What might a space on a market map indicate?	An unmet demand
12	State two features often used to label market map axes.	Two from: price / quality / ease of use / level of innovation

Previous questions

Use the questions below to check your knowledge from previous chapters.

Questions / Answers

#	Question	Answer
1	State two ways to identify customer needs.	Personal experience; spotting opportunities
2	Market research is the process of collecting and analysing information from what three key areas?	Market; competitors; customers
3	State two purposes of market research.	Two from: to help businesses identify and understand customer needs / to help businesses identify gaps in the market / to help businesses reduce risk / to inform business decisions

Practice

Exam-style questions

5.1 Which *one* of the following is related to the lifestyle of a customer? **(1)**

    A Activities   **C** Gender

    B Income   **D** Age

5.2 Which *two* of the following are categories used to identify market segments? **(2)**

    A Demographics   **D** Product

    B Price   **E** Place

    C Lifestyle

5.3 Explain *one* way in which primary research can help segment markets. **(3)**

5.4 Discuss the importance of market mapping for identifying gaps in the market. **(6)**

ABC Motorcycles Ltd is a motorcycle manufacturer based in Birmingham. It is known for its low-cost mopeds, which are popular with men in their early twenties because they are fuel efficient and easy to personalise and modify.

ABC Motorcycles Ltd is keen to expand its customer base because it is concerned it is dependent on one market segment. It has developed an electric moped, but is not sure who the target market should be. It has developed a market map (Figure 1) to help in its decision-making.

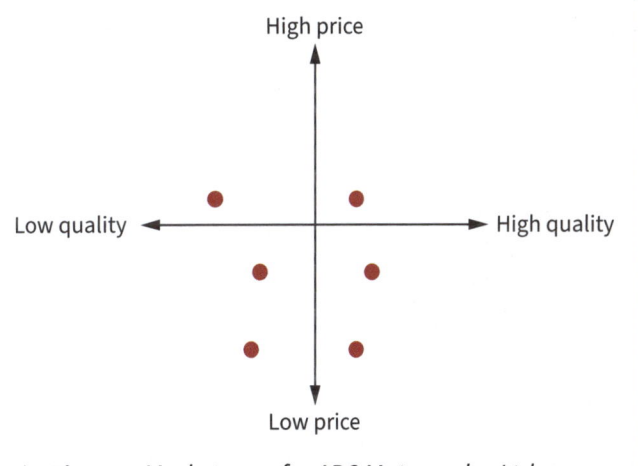

▲ **Figure 1** Market map for ABC Motorcycles Ltd

5.5 State *one* impact to ABC Motorcycles Ltd of segmenting the market. **(1)**

5.6 Outline *one* drawback to ABC Motorcycles Ltd of relying on one market segment. **(2)**

5.7 Analyse the impact of ABC Motorcycles Ltd focussing on income when segmenting the market. **(6)**

5.8 In order to access a new market segment, ABC Motorcycles Ltd is considering two options:

    Option 1: high price and high quality

    Option 2: low price and high quality.

    Justify which *one* of these two options ABC Motorcycles Ltd should choose. **(9)**

> **EXAM TIP**
>
> When thinking about market segmentation, remember to use knowledge from previous chapters that may be relevant, such as the impact of changes on what customers want and the impact of products becoming obsolete.

Knowledge

6 The competitive environment

Competition

A business will almost always face competition for customers in the market. There are two types of competitors:

Direct competitors
Other businesses that sell a similar product to the same target customer at a similar price.

Indirect competitors
Businesses that sell a **substitute** product. This substitute satisfies the same want or need and it is targeted at the same customer, but may not be a similar price.

Understanding the competitive environment

To understand the competitive environment, a business must know about the wants and needs of the target market, and the strengths and weaknesses of competitors. This will allow it to:

- select the most appropriate **marketing mix**
- differentiate the brand or product from its competition
- understand how difficult and expensive it is to enter the marketplace as a new competitor.

Strengths and weaknesses of competitors

Strengths and weaknesses of competitors can include:

Quality
For example, having a higher quality product than a competitor could be a strength if customers value quality over other factors.

Product range
For example, having a wider range of products than competitors is usually a strength because it gives customers more choice.

Price
For example, charging more than a competitor for a very similar product is a weakness if customers are price-sensitive.

Location
For example, selecting a location that is more convenient for customers is a strength as it could attract more customers.

Customer service
For example, poor customer service – being slow or rude to customers – is a weakness because it can impact on reputation and encourage customers to move to the competition.

The impact of competition on business decision-making

Competition has many impacts on business decision-making. A business must consider how competition impacts things such as customer behaviour and profit. For example:

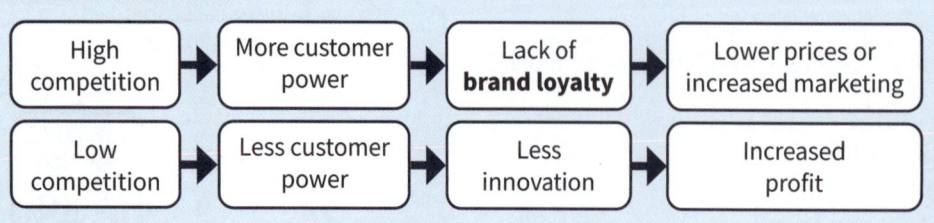

 **Key terms** Make sure you can write a definition for these key terms

brand loyalty
marketing mix
substitute

Retrieval

6

Answer the questions below. Cover the answers column with a piece of paper and write down as many answers as you can. Check and repeat.

Questions | Answers

1 What must a business know about in order to understand the competitive environment?

The wants and needs of the target market, and the strengths and weaknesses of competitors

2 What will understanding the competitive environment allow a business to do?

One from: select the most appropriate marketing mix / differentiate the brand or product from its competition / understand how difficult and expensive it is to enter the marketplace as a new competitor

3 Identify one aspect a business should consider when thinking about the strengths and weaknesses of competitors.

One from: price / quality / location / product range / customer service

4 State one impact of high competition on business decision-making.

Lower prices or increased marketing

Previous questions

Use the questions below to check your knowledge from previous chapters.

Questions | Answers

1 Identify two categories used to segment a market.

One from: location / demographics / lifestyle / income / age

2 State two features often used to label market map axes.

Two from: price / quality / ease of use / level of innovation

Practice

Exam-style questions

6.1 Explain *one* way in which a high-quality product could be a weakness for a business. **(3)**

6.2 Discuss the importance of considering the competition when making business decisions. **(6)**

Practice

Exam-style questions

Seasonal Windows Ltd is a family-owned business that first opened in Manchester in 2005. Its customers include premium retailers who require sustainable, seasonal displays in their shop windows, as well as wealthy families who host private parties.

Seasonal Windows Ltd offers a very specialised service. It designs and builds the window displays, maintains them while they are in place, and then removes and cleans up afterwards.

Seasonal Windows Ltd prides itself on understanding its customers' needs, carrying out extensive primary and secondary research to understand the newest trends to inform its business decisions. Its advertising is targeted at its specific market segments.

Seasonal Windows Ltd uses social media extensively, both to promote the business and for market research. The business has now grown from a local business to a regional business, and it now serves the needs of customers throughout the north of England, from Liverpool to Leeds.

Non-financial aims have become increasingly important to its customers, which has led Seasonal Windows Ltd to build relationships with local suppliers so it can be more sustainable as a business.

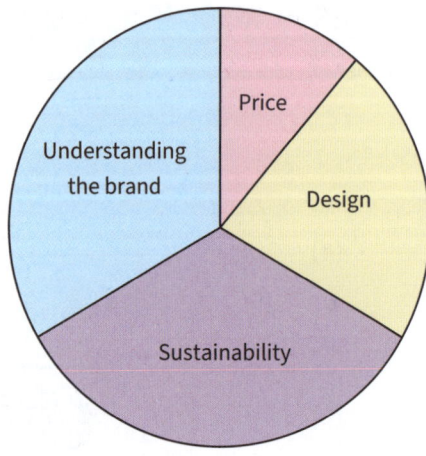

◀ **Figure 1** *The factors Seasonal Windows Ltd's customers consider most important when making purchasing decisions*

6.3 State *one* customer need Seasonal Windows Ltd must consider. **(1)**

6.4 State *one* method of primary market research Seasonal Windows Ltd could use. **(1)**

6.5 Using the information in Figure 1, identify the factor which is least important for Seasonal Windows Ltd's customers. **(1)**

6.6 Outline *one* purpose of secondary market research for Seasonal Windows Ltd. **(2)**

> **EXAM TIP**
> When answering 'Outline' questions, you must refer to something in the case study.

6.7 Outline *one* advantage to Seasonal Windows Ltd of understanding its customers' brands. **(2)**

6.8 As a result of data gathered during primary market research, Seasonal Windows Ltd has identified a new trend: digital elements in window displays. Analyse the risk to Seasonal Windows Ltd of investing in the new technology required. **(6)**

6.9 In order to meet the needs of its customers better, Seasonal Windows Ltd is considering two market research options:

Option 1: an online questionnaire to collect quantitative data

Option 2: a focus group to collect qualitative data.

Justify which *one* of these two options Seasonal Windows Ltd should choose. **(9)**

> **EXAM TIP**
> 'Evaluate' questions do not have a definitive answer. However, the likely impact must be based on evidence from the case study. Ensure that you provide both positive and negative impacts, backed by evidence from the case study, to show a balanced evaluation.

6.10 Evaluate the likely impacts on Seasonal Windows Ltd of understanding the competitive environment when making business decisions. You should use the information provided as well as your knowledge of business. **(12)**

6 Practice

# Knowledge

7 Business aims and objectives

Defining business aims and objectives

Business aims and objectives are the goals and targets a business sets itself. They provide focus for stakeholders. Aims and objectives change as businesses grow and develop.

REVISION TIP
SMART targets are Specific, Measurable, Achievable, Realistic, and Timebound.

Aims
- Overall goals or ambitions
- Broad, general, and apply to all areas of the business
- Form a long-term strategy

Objectives
- **SMART targets** used by business leaders to track progress
- Each objective focuses on a particular business area
- Each business area may have many objectives
- Often short term

Business aims and objectives when starting up

Aims and objectives can be divided into two main categories: financial aims and objectives, and non-financial aims and objectives.

1. Financial aims and objectives

Start-up businesses cannot survive without sufficient finance, so they often have similar financial aims and objectives:

Aim	Example objectives
Survival	Survive the first year Have finance available to ensure positive monthly cash flow
Profit	Reach **profitability** within the first two years of trading Increase profits by 7% per year from year three
Sales	Sell 5000 products in first six months of trading
Market share	Achieve 1% **market share** in Manchester in one year
Financial security	Achieve and maintain a financial surplus of £25,000 by the end of the financial year Establish credit facilities to the value of £10,000 for five years

2. Non-financial aims and objectives

Non-financial aims and objectives are more likely to differ from business to business, because they depend on the nature of the business. They are often less precise and more aspirational than financial objectives, and could include:

Categories	Example aims	Example objectives
Social	Ethical practices	Ensure a minimum of 50% of materials used in **business operations** are sustainable
	Environmental concerns	Reduce the use of fossil fuels by 50% by 2030
Personal satisfaction	Meet personal success criteria	Ensure the business can sustain my desired lifestyle
Challenge	Meet aspirational targets	Become the number one **supplier** in the east of England by the end of year three
Independence	Make all key business decisions	Set business hours to meet personal needs Personally select suppliers and set selling prices
Control	Ownership	Retain control of the business Decide the direction of the business

Why aims and objectives differ between businesses

Aims and objectives differ from business to business, for internal and external reasons. Influencing factors can include business size, level of competition, type of business and business culture.

Business size
Smaller businesses may decide to **profit satisfice**: they set a minimum acceptable level of profit instead of maximising potential financial gains.
Larger businesses may decide to try to grow market share or profit.
Businesses in **saturated markets** may decide to expand nationally or internationally. A saturated market is a market where there are no more possible customers for a product.

Business culture
Established businesses and family-owned businesses may decide to prioritise long-term stability over profit.
New businesses may decide to prioritise short-term profitability if the life of the product is limited.

Level of competition
High levels of competition may make survival more important than social aims.
Low levels of competition may encourage a business to try to grow market share or profit.

Type of business
Owners of different types of businesses have different expectations depending on their size and structure. A sole trader may try to profit satisfice, while a private limited company may decide to try to grow market share. A public limited company may decide to try to maximise profits to increase **shareholder** returns.
Not-for-profit organisations often focus on social aims and objectives.

> **REVISION TIP**
> Instead of revising by yourself, try working with a study buddy. You are more likely to feel motivated if your revision has a social aspect to it.

Key terms — Make sure you can write a definition for these key terms:
business operation, market share, profitability, profit satisfice, saturated market, shareholder, SMART target, supplier

Retrieval

Answer the questions below. Cover the answers column with a piece of paper and write down as many answers as you can. Check and repeat.

Questions | Answers

1. What is the difference between an aim and an objective? | An aim is an overall goal or ambition that forms part of a long-term strategy; an aim is broad, general, and applies to all areas of the business. An objective is a SMART target used by business leaders to track progress, which is often short-term; an objective focuses on a particular business area, and each business area may have many objectives

2. What does SMART stand for in 'SMART target'? | Specific, Measurable, Achievable, Realistic, and Timebound

3. Why do start-up businesses often have similar financial aims and objectives? | They cannot survive without sufficient finance

4. Name two financial aims and objectives. | Two from: survival / profit / sales / market share / financial security

5. Why are non-financial aims and objectives more likely to differ from business to business? | Because they depend on the nature of the business

6. Name two non-financial aims and objectives. | Two from: social / personal satisfaction / challenge / independence / control

7. Aims and objectives differ from business to business. Give one factor that influences this. | One from: business size / level of competition / type of business / business culture

8. What is profit satisficing? | Setting a minimum acceptable level of profit instead of maximising potential gains

9. Do high or low levels of competition make survival more important than social aims? | High levels of competition

10. Do not-for-profit organisations often focus on financial or social aims and objectives? | Social

Previous questions

Use the questions below to check your knowledge from previous chapters.

Questions | Answers

1. State two ways in which demographics group people. | Two from: age / stage of life / gender / level of education / religion / family size / income

2. What must a business know about in order to understand the competitive environment? | The wants and needs of the target market, and the strengths and weaknesses of competitors

3. State one impact of high competition on business decision-making. | Lower prices or increased marketing

7 Business aims and objectives

Practice 7

Exam-style questions

7.1 Which *one* of the following describes an aim? (1)

- **A** Used to inform long-term strategy
- **B** Focused on one business area
- **C** SMART
- **D** Short-term

7.2 Which *two* of the following are the focus of financial aims and objectives? (2)

- **A** Challenge
- **B** Market share
- **C** Society
- **D** Control
- **E** Profit

7.3 Explain *one* market segment an entrepreneur might target. (3)

7.4 Discuss the importance of considering business size when setting aims and objectives. (6)

Bubble Tea Ltd sells bubble tea, a mix of tea, milk and fruit juices containing chewy tapioca balls. It is very popular in larger cities where there are many international visitors, and it is targeted at teenagers who want a refreshing alternative to carbonated drinks. The company's original aim was profit satisficing.

Joe, the owner, wants Bubble Tea Ltd to be the number one brand in the UK, with a cafe in every major city. Bubble Tea Ltd currently has ten profitable takeaway cafes in larger cities, with limited seating to keep costs low. Competition is high. Joe is considering growing the business by targeting smaller cities where competition is either very low or does not exist. Joe has been told that he is unlikely to achieve his aim of growth by other bubble tea cafe owners.

7.5 Give *one* example of a business aim. (1)

7.6 Outline *one* benefit to Bubble Tea Ltd of using questionnaires to assess customer demand in smaller cities. (2)

7.7 Outline one way that low competition in smaller cities could impact Bubble Tea Ltd's aim. (2)

7.8 Bubble Tea Ltd must decide between two options:

Option 1: continue to pursue its aim of growth by targeting smaller cities

Option 2: remain in larger cities and focus on non-financial aims.

Justify which *one* of these two options Bubble Tea Ltd should choose. (9)

> **EXAM TIP**
>
> When answering 'Outline' questions, identify the benefit or impact stated or hinted at in the case study for one mark, and provide context from the case study for the second mark.

Knowledge

8 Business revenues, costs and profits

Financial concepts

To succeed, a business needs to make a profit. To make a profit, entrepreneurs need to understand financial concepts. They need to use calculations to plan business activity and make the best possible decisions.

Understanding financial concepts

Revenue

Revenue, also known as 'income', is the total amount of money made from business operations.

A business must ensure it has enough revenue from sales, interest on savings and/or selling franchises to ensure its survival.

A successful business forecasts (predicts) revenue to create a **budget** (an estimate of income and expenditure for a set period of time in the future). This helps it decide the quantity of **raw materials** to order, and ensures there is enough **cash** in the business to meet planned costs.

Calculating revenue

(sales) revenue = price × quantity

> **EXAM TIP**
>
> In your exams, you might find 'revenue', 'sales revenue', and even 'total revenue' used interchangeably.

Costs

Fixed costs are costs that do not vary with the level of output; they *do not* change however many products are made.

Variable costs are costs that vary with the level of output; they *do* change with the number of products made. This means that variable costs depend on how much a business can afford after paying all fixed costs.

Total costs are fixed costs plus variable costs, and a business needs to know its total costs to plan accurately. If its total costs are higher than its forecasted revenue, it must organise a short-term **overdraft** or a long-term bank **loan**.

Calculating costs

total cost (TC) = total fixed costs (TFC) + total variable costs (TVC)

Examples of fixed costs include insurance, rent, tax, and wages and salaries.

Examples of variable costs include raw materials, packaging, utilities, **commission**, and hourly labour.

Profit and loss

Most businesses aim to make a profit, although entrepreneurs and new businesses often make a loss in the first years of trading. A loss is shown in brackets, and it means costs are higher than revenue.

Gross profit or loss is the revenue a business has left after deducting the costs of making and selling its goods and services. This means revenue is higher than the **cost of sales** (higher than the cost of the raw materials used to produce the goods or services sold).

Net profit or loss is a more realistic representation of profits. It is the revenue a business has left after deducting all its costs.

Calculating profit and loss

gross profit (or loss) = sales revenue − cost of sales

net profit (or loss) = gross profit − other **operating expenses** and interest

Operating expenses are the ongoing expenses required for maintaining a business's day-to-day operational activities.

Interest

Interest can be a cost and/or a revenue stream for a business:

- When a business borrows money from a bank, interest is the cost of borrowing.
- When a business saves money with a bank, interest is a form of revenue received.

Calculating interest

$$\text{interest (on loans) in \%} = \frac{\text{total amount repaid} - \text{borrowed amount}}{\text{borrowed amount}} \times 100$$

Break-even level of output

The **break-even point** is the point where the revenue a business generates equals all its costs; the point at which there is no profit and no loss.

Calculating the break-even point helps a business understand the minimum number of sales needed to cover its costs: this is the **break-even level of output**.

Although a start-up business may set break even as its initial aim, a business must make a profit in the long term.

Calculating break-even level of output

$$\text{break-even point in units} = \frac{\text{fixed costs}}{(\text{sales price} - \text{variable costs})}$$

break-even point in costs/revenue = break-even point in units × sales price

Margin of safety

The **margin of safety** is the difference between a business's break-even point and its maximum possible output. It shows the level of profit a business can make.

Knowing the margin of safety helps a business set sales targets. Sales targets must be:

- above the break-even point, to allow a profit to be made
- below the maximum possible output, because it is not possible to sell more than can be made.

Calculating margin of safety

margin of safety = actual or budgeted sales − break-even sales

Knowledge

8 Business revenues, costs and profits

Interpreting break-even diagrams

Break-even diagrams plot costs and revenue on a graph. They help businesses analyse:

- the impact of changes in revenue and costs
- the break-even level of output
- the margin of safety
- profit and loss.

Break-even diagrams are predictions based on experience and past data. Therefore, entrepreneurs with new businesses often have to guess many of the variable costs.

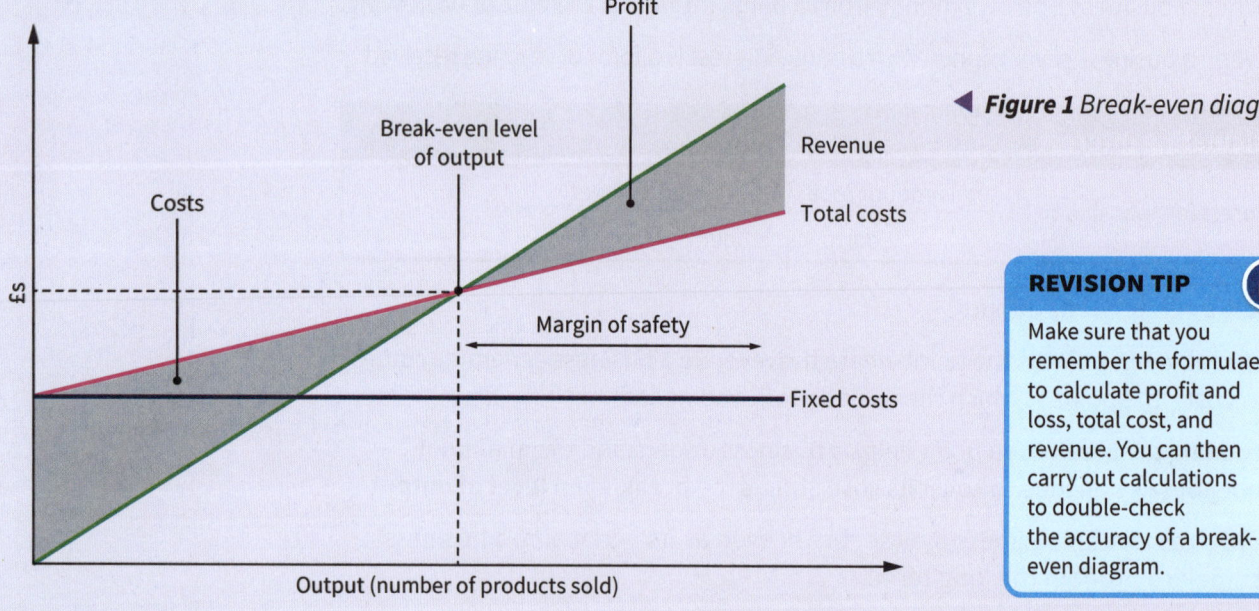

◀ **Figure 1** Break-even diagram

REVISION TIP

Make sure that you remember the formulae to calculate profit and loss, total cost, and revenue. You can then carry out calculations to double-check the accuracy of a break-even diagram.

The impact of changes in revenue and costs

Break-even diagrams can help businesses calculate the likely impact of changes in revenue and costs.

Lower-than-expected revenue and / or higher-than-expected costs are likely to have negative impacts, which include:

- ✗ a reduction in gross profit, which reduces the margin of safety
- ✗ an increase in the cost of **promotion**, in an attempt to increase demand
- ✗ a reduction in the budget available to cover costs, which could lead to a reduction in quality and the cost of raw materials.

Higher-than-expected revenue and / or lower-than-expected costs are likely to have positive impacts, which include:

- ✓ an increase in gross profit, which means the business has more money to spend on things such as research and development, and promotion.

8

Break-even level of output

The break-even level of output shows the point where revenue is equal to costs.

Knowing the break-even level of output allows a business to:

- set the minimum number of sales required at a particular price point to cover costs
- calculate different margins of safety by adjusting sales forecasts and costs.

Margin of safety

The margin of safety shows the level of profit a business can make at a certain level of sales. The risk of making a loss reduces the larger the margin of safety is.

Profit and loss

Break-even diagrams show profit and loss.

- Profit is shown when the break-even point is passed, when total revenue is higher than total costs.
- Loss is shown when the break-even point has not been reached, when total costs are higher than total revenue.

Key terms Make sure you can write a definition for these key terms

break-even level of output   break-even point   budget   cash   commission   cost of sale   fixed cost   gross profit or loss   interest   loan   margin of safety   net profit or loss   operating expenses   overdraft   promotion   raw material   total cost   variable cost

8 Knowledge

Retrieval

Answer the questions below. Cover the answers column with a piece of paper and write down as many answers as you can. Check and repeat.

Questions / Answers

#	Question	Answer
1	What is 'revenue'?	The total amount of money made from a business's operations
2	Why does a successful business forecast revenue to create a budget?	It helps to decide the quantity of raw materials to order, and ensure there is enough cash in the business to meet planned costs
3	Why can fixed costs be forecasted accurately?	They do not vary with the level of output; they do not change however many products are made
4	Name the two types of profit a business can make.	Gross profit; net profit
5	What do businesses use income statements for?	To keep track of revenue and costs to show profit levels
6	What is the break-even point?	The point where the revenue a business generates equals all its costs
7	What is the margin of safety?	The difference between a business's break-even point and its maximum possible output
8	What is the formula for calculating revenue?	(sales) revenue = price × quantity
9	What is the formula for calculating the break-even point in units?	break-even point in units = $\dfrac{\text{fixed costs}}{\text{(sales price – variable cost)}}$
10	Name two things break-even diagrams help businesses to analyse.	Two from: the impact of changes in revenue and costs / the break-even level of output / the margin of safety / profit and loss
11	Identify one possible outcome of lower-than-expected costs.	An increase in gross profit, which means the business has more money to spend on things such as research and development, and promotion

Previous questions

Use the questions below to check your knowledge from previous chapters.

#	Question	Answer
1	Identify one aspect a business should consider when thinking about the strengths and weaknesses of competitors.	One from: price / quality / location / product range / customer service
2	Name two non-financial aims and objectives.	Two from: social / personal satisfaction / challenge / independence / control
3	Name two financial aims and objectives.	Two from: survival / profit / sales / market share / financial security

8 Business revenues, costs and profits

Practice

Exam-style questions

8.1 Which *two* of the following are fixed costs? (2)

    A Raw materials   **D** Salaries

    B Packaging   **E** Wages

    C Rent

8.2 Explain *one* benefit of creating a budget for an entrepreneur. (3)

8.3 Explain one reason why it is is important for an entrepreneur to understand the competitive environment. (3)

8.4 Discuss the importance of calculating the break-even point when setting the selling price of a product. (6)

Couple of Quid Ltd sells all its products for £2. Caleb, the majority shareholder, has identified a new product he thinks will be popular.

A branded version of the product is already popular, but very expensive. However, Caleb has sourced an unbranded version, which costs £1.75 per unit to buy. The minimum order is 8000. The shop must sell a minimum of 6000 units within a two-month period to make the minimum level of profit required. There is currently very little competition for the unbranded version.

Caleb has produced a break-even diagram (Figure 1), showing the break-even point and the margin of safety.

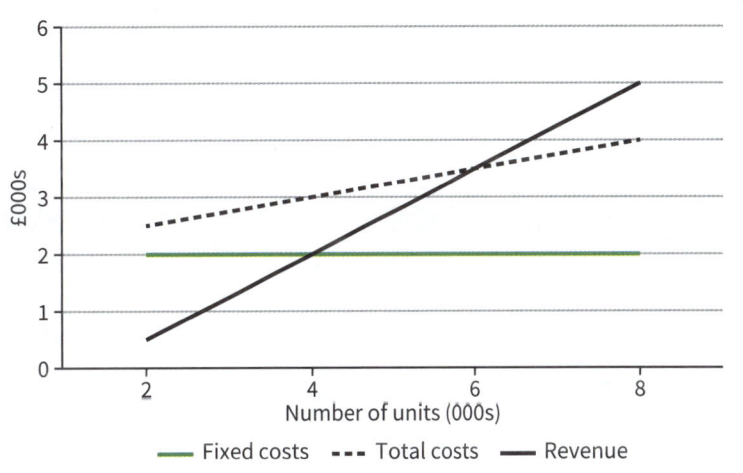

▲ Figure 1

8.5 Give *one* example of a variable cost. (1)

8.6 Using the information in Figure 1, calculate Couple of Quid Ltd's margin of safety. (2)

EXAM TIP

Add labels to, and shade relevant areas of, a break-even diagram before answering questions about it. This will help you visualise your answers.

8.7 Outline *one* potential impact of increased competition on Couple of Quid Ltd. (2)

8.8 Couple of Quid Ltd must now decide between two options:

    Option 1: choose to sell the new product

    Option 2: choose not to sell the new product.

    Justify which *one* of these two options Couple of Quid Ltd should choose. (9)

Knowledge

9 Cash and cash flow

Cash

Businesses must have cash to pay day-to-day expenses. Cash is money that is easily available as coins and notes or in online accounts.

Cash flows into a business from revenue and out of a business to people and organisations owed money.

The importance of cash to a business

A business must manage its cash flow effectively to operate efficiently.

1. A business needs cash to pay suppliers, overheads and employees

- It is important to have a good relationship with suppliers and a key element is paying suppliers on time. A good relationship means goods arrive on time and in perfect condition.
- **Overheads** must be paid on time. These are business expenses not directly related to creating a product, such as rent. If overheads are not paid promptly they may be withdrawn by service providers.
- Employees must be paid on time. The additional costs associated with employees – such as National Insurance contributions and tax deductions – must also be paid on time. If employees are not paid promptly they will often look for more secure jobs and vital skills could be lost.

2. A business needs cash to prevent business failure (insolvency)

When more cash leaves a business than comes in during a given period it has **negative cash flow**. A business with negative cash flow can become **insolvent**: it can fail because it is unable to pay its **debts**.

Even a profitable business may become insolvent. If a business's **debtors** do not pay their debts on time the business may find that it is unable to pay its **creditors** on time.

A business tries to remain **solvent** by ensuring **positive cash flow** by:
- obtaining **credit** from banks, such as an overdraft to cover short-term negative cash flow
- ensuring the credit given to customers is for a shorter period than the credit provided by suppliers
- limiting the number of customers who pay by credit to those who have proven themselves to be trustworthy and ensuring there are more customers who pay cash on delivery.

3. A business needs to understand the difference between cash and profit

Cash is the money that flows in to a business from sales and out of the business when paying bills. Profit is revenue received minus total costs.

Businesses often fail when entrepreneurs do not budget carefully and spend their cash without considering how and when costs are going be paid.

Cash-flow forecasts

A **cash-flow forecast** predicts the amount of cash that will flow into and out of a business in a set time period, which helps it know if it can pay its costs at the appropriate time.

It is more difficult for an entrepreneur to prepare a cash-flow forecast as they are unlikely to have historical data they can use to predict cash inflows and cash outflows. This means a start-up's cash-flow forecasts may not be realistic.

As a result entrepreneurs must monitor cash flow very carefully and adjust their projections frequently to make sure they are as accurate as possible.

Interpreting cash-flow forecasts

Cash-flow forecasts are often calculated monthly and created using spreadsheets so data can be changed and totals update automatically.

There are five main areas of a cash-flow forecast.

> **REVISION TIP**
>
> Although many students think finance and accounting is difficult it is something that people do every day. Think of yourself as a business and create your own cash-flow forecast estimating how much money you will receive from for example parents or guardians and part-time jobs and how much you want to spend on for example activities and clothes. Do you have enough coming in to cover your costs?

Cash inflows

Cash inflows records all the cash flowing into a business. Businesses may wish to be cautious when predicting future income by predicting lower-than-expected sales.

Net cash flow

Net cash flow is the difference between cash inflows and cash outflows. The formula is:

net cash flow = cash inflows – cash outflows in a given period

Net cash flow will vary each month as cash inflows and outflows rise and fall. Businesses must try to ensure that if a negative cash flow is predicted there will be enough cash in reserve to cover costs.

	Jan (£)	Feb (£)	Mar (£)
Cash inflows			
Sales	9000	4000	12,000
Total inflows	9000	4000	12,000
Cash outflows			
Wages	2000	1000	3000
Salaries	1000	1000	1000
Marketing	1500	500	2000
Rent	2000	2000	2000
Raw materials	1500	750	2000
Total outflows	8000	5250	10,000
Net cash flow	1000	(1250)	2000
Opening balance	0	1000	(250)
Closing balance	1000	(250)	1750

Cash outflows

Cash outflows records all the ways in which money leaves a business. Businesses often predict higher-than-expected costs to ensure the budget can accommodate an unexpected rise in costs.

Opening balance

The **opening balance** is the amount of money a business has available as cash (either in hand or in a bank account) at the beginning of each period. The formula is:

opening balance = closing balance of the previous period

Closing balance

The **closing balance** is the amount of money a business has available as cash (either in hand or in a bank account) at the end of each period. The formula is:

closing balance = opening balance + net cash flow

Key terms — Make sure you can write a definition for these key terms

cash-flow forecast   closing balance   credit   creditor
debt   debtor   insolvent   negative cash flow   net cash flow
opening balance   overhead   positive cash flow   solvent

Retrieval

Answer the questions below. Cover the answers column with a piece of paper and write down as many answers as you can. Check and repeat.

	Questions	Answers
1	Why must businesses have cash available?	To pay day-to-day expenses
2	Where do businesses keep cash?	In a bank account or in hand in the form of notes and coins
3	Give three reasons why cash is important to a business.	A business needs cash to pay suppliers, overheads and employees; a business needs cash to prevent business failure (insolvency); a business needs to understand the difference between cash and profit
4	Why is it important to pay employees promptly?	If employees are not paid promptly they will often look for more secure jobs and vital skills could be lost
5	When does a business have negative cash flow?	When more cash leaves the business than comes in during a given period
6	What happens if a business has negative cash flow?	It does not have enough cash available to pay its bills when needed and it can become insolvent
7	What is the difference between cash and profit?	Cash is the money that flows in to a business from sales and out of the business when paying bills. Profit is revenue received minus total costs
8	What does a cash-flow forecast predict?	The amount of cash that will flow into and out of a business in a set time period
9	Why is it more difficult for an entrepreneur to create a cash-flow forecast?	Entrepreneurs are unlikely to have historical data they can use to predict cash inflows and cash outflows
10	What is the formula for net cash flow?	net cash flow = cash inflows – cash outflows in a given period
11	What is the opening balance on a cash-flow forecast?	The amount of money a business has available as cash (either in hand or in a bank account) at the beginning of each period

Previous questions

Use the questions below to check your knowledge from previous chapters.

	Questions	Answers
1	Name two non-financial aims and objectives.	Two from: social / personal satisfaction / challenge / independence / control
2	What do businesses use income statements for?	To keep track of revenue and costs to show profit levels
3	Name the two types of profit a business can make.	Gross profit; net profit

9 Cash and cash flow

Practice

Exam-style questions

9.1 Which *one* of the following is a cash inflow? (1)

  A Payments to suppliers   C Overheads
  B Paying employees   D Revenue

9.2 Explain *one* benefit of cash-flow forecasts to an entrepreneur. (3)

9.3 Explain *one* benefit of achieving a break-even level of output for a business. (3)

9.4 Discuss the importance to a business of calculating net cash flow when creating a budget. (6)

Fred's Flowers is located in Rotherham. Fred the owner of the business has been importing and selling flowers from Europe for five years. He has a good reputation for quality and price and has a steady income from weddings and funerals.

Fred is concerned about a new 10% tax that is being introduced on imports from Europe in June. Fred has created a cash-flow forecast for the two months from May (see Table 1) to help him understand the possible impact of the tax on his cash flow.

▶ **Table 1** Fred's Flowers' cash-flow forecast

	May (£)	June (£)
Cash inflows		
Sales	10,000	10,000
Total inflows	**10,000**	**10,000**
Cash outflows		
Fixed costs	2000	2000
Variable costs	3000	3300
Total outflows	**5000**	**5300**
Net cash flow	5000	4700
Opening balance	3000	(ii)
Closing balance	(i)	12,700

9.5 Using the information in Table 1, calculate the value of (i) and (ii). (2)

EXAM TIP
When looking at cash-flow forecasts the closing balance of the first period should match the opening balance of the next period. If they are different there is a mistake somewhere.

9.6 Outline *one* benefit of using a cash-flow forecast to understand the impact of the new tax on Fred's Flowers. (2)

9.7 Analyse the impact on Fred's Flowers of a 50% drop in sales in May and June. (6)

9.8 Fred's Flowers must now decide between two options:

  Option 1: increase prices
  Option 2: decrease expected profit.
  Justify which *one* of these two options Fred's Flowers should choose. (9)

Knowledge

10 Sources of business finance

Short-term sources of finance

Short-term sources of finance should be used to maintain positive cash flow. They are designed to be paid off in weeks or months, and are mainly used to:

- cover costs incurred during the production process, before products are sold
- cover unexpected costs or emergencies.

Overdrafts

An overdraft is a pre-arranged credit agreement with a bank, which allows a business to borrow money up to a pre-agreed limit at an agreed interest rate.

Advantages and disadvantages

✓ Flexibility: only used when businesses do not have enough money available to pay bills ✓ Speed: easy to arrange and available whenever needed	✗ Limited: you can usually borrow only small sums of money ✗ Expensive: interest rates on overdrafts are often much higher than interest rates on bank loans

Trade credit

Trade credit is a pre-arranged credit agreement with a supplier, allowing a business to purchase goods and services from the supplier and pay by a specified later date.

Advantages and disadvantages

✓ Cash flow: receiving goods and services before paying for them helps cash flow. Trade credit agreements often become more generous over time, as the two businesses come to trust each other. ✓ Low cost: they are often interest-free until the repayment date.	✗ Requires trust: suppliers often limit trade credit for unknown customers, and it takes time to build trust. ✗ Risky if terms are not met: interest rates can be high and the relationship with the supplier can quickly be damaged if payments are not made on time. Failing to meet the terms of trade credit can also result in a supplier refusing to deliver goods and services.

Long-term sources of finance

Long-term sources of finance are often used for **capital investment**. They are designed to be paid off over long periods of time, over years, not weeks or months.

Personal savings

When a business owner invests their own money into their business, they are using their personal savings as a source of finance. This is also known as 'owner's capital'.

Advantages and disadvantages

✓ Retain control: there are no rules set on what the money can be used for. ✓ Low cost: no interest payments are required.	✗ Limited: the size of the loan is dependent on the amount of personal savings available. ✗ Impact on well-being: when a business owner loans their business money, it reduces the amount of money they have available to meet their personal needs.

Venture capital

Venture capital is an investment made by a larger business or a successful entrepreneur into a start-up business, in return for a share of the business.

Advantages and disadvantages

- ✓ Risk tolerance: venture capitalists are willing to invest in high-risk start-up businesses.
- ✓ Expertise: venture capitalists often provide specific knowledge and expertise in addition to finance.
- ✗ Loss of ownership: the venture capitalist take a percentage of the business's profits.
- ✗ Loss of control: as a shareholder, the venture capitalist can influence decisions.

Share capital

Businesses can sell shares to raise **share capital**. Shareholders are eligible for a share of profits and have voting rights.

Advantages and disadvantages

- ✓ Large sums: it can raise large sums of money quickly.
- ✓ Low cost: there is no requirement to repay the share capital raised and no interest payments.
- ✗ Loss of ownership: shareholders take a percentage of a business's profits.
- ✗ Loss of control: selling more than 50% of the business will lead to the original owner losing control.

Loans

A loan is a specified amount of money borrowed from a bank, which is paid back with interest over a set period of time. Loans can be secured against a physical asset, such as a building.

Advantages and disadvantages

- ✓ Speed: it is quick and easy to arrange, especially for successful businesses that have physical **assets**.
- ✓ Cash flow: the cost of the repayments and the duration of the loan are known, so it is easy to budget.
- ✓ No loss of control as long as the loan is repaid, a business owner does not lose control.
- ✗ Cost: Interest must be paid regularly, even if the business does not make a profit.
- ✗ Credit checks: a bank will investigate to ensure the business is able to make the repayments. If it has doubts, they may offer less money or insist that the loan is secured against a business asset.

Retained profit

Successful businesses make profits from business activities. When this profit is retained within the business, it can be used for capital investment.

Advantages and disadvantages

- ✓ Low cost: there is no requirement to repay **retained profit** and no interest payments.
- ✓ Speed: retained profit is instantly available.
- ✓ No loss of control: a business owner does not lose control of their business.
- ✗ Limited: the amount of money available depends on the profit made in previous years. Start-up businesses do not have any retained profit available.
- ✗ Opportunity cost: shareholders may want, or need, retained profit to be paid as **dividends**.

Knowledge

10 Sources of business finance

Crowd funding

Crowd funding is raising small amounts of capital from many investors, who are often given a limited reward (such as a discount or a free product) and not a share of the business.

Advantages and disadvantages

- ✓ No loss of control: a business owner does not lose control of their business.
- ✓ Quick and easy: the internet makes it easy for many people to pledge capital, and for businesses to raise money quickly.

- ✗ High chance of failure because a business must persuade many people to believe in the future success of its product.
- ✗ Risky: allows competitors early sight of ideas, which could be copied. The business could lose the competitive edge it would have gained from being the first to market.

REVISION TIP

You can find out more about internal and external sources of finance for established and growing businesses in Chapter 20.

 **Key terms** — Make sure you can write a definition for these key terms: asset, capital investment, crowd funding, dividend, retained profit, share capital, trade credit, venture capital

Retrieval

10

Answer the questions below. Cover the answers column with a piece of paper and write down as many answers as you can. Check and repeat.

Questions | Answers

1 What should short-term sources of finance be used for? | To maintain positive cash flow

2 Give one advantage of an overdraft. | One from: flexibility (only used when businesses do not have enough money available to pay bills) / speed (easy to arrange and available whenever needed)

3 What are long-term sources of finance often used for? | Capital investment

4 Are long-term sources of finance designed to be paid off over years or over weeks or months? | Years

5 Give one advantage of using personal savings as a long-term source of finance. | One from: retain control (there are no rules set on what the money can be used for) / low cost (no interest payments are required)

6 Identify one long-term source of finance that results in a business owner losing control over their business. | One from: venture capital / share capital

7 State one disadvantage of venture capital as a long-term source of finance. | One from: loss of ownership (the venture capitalist takes a percentage of the business's profits) / loss of control (as a shareholder, the venture capitalist has the ability to influence decisions in ways that may not benefit the original owner)

8 State one reason why crowd funding is advantageous as a long-term source of finance. | One from: no loss of control (a business owner does not lose control of their business) / quick and easy (the internet makes it easy for many people to pledge capital and for businesses to raise large sums of money quickly)

Previous questions

Use the questions below to check your knowledge from previous chapters.

Questions | Answers

1 Why can fixed costs be forecasted accurately? | They do not vary with the level of output; they do not change however many products are made

2 Give three reasons why cash is important to a business. | A business needs cash to pay suppliers, overheads and employees; a business needs cash to prevent business failure (insolvency); a business needs to understand the difference between cash and profit

3 What is the difference between cash and profit? | Cash is the money that flows in to a business from sales, and out of the business when paying bills. Profit is revenue received minus total costs

Exam-style questions

Fried Fries plc is the largest producer of fries in Europe. It is also the largest supplier of fries to fast-food chains and supermarkets in Europe, with 12 factories across the continent. Fried Fries plc employs 4000 people across all its sites. It is in the process of upgrading the production lines in its factories, using technology to improve efficiency. It is funding this upgrade with loans. To date, six factories have been upgraded.

Fried Fries plc has recently been in national newspapers because it has made 10% of its staff redundant, closed two of its older factories, and reduced the working hours of remaining staff by up to 20%.

A recent press release has highlighted falling sales because Fried Fries plc's largest customer, Benny's Burgers, has reduced purchases by 20%. Benny's Burgers has identified a new trend: more and more customers are ordering healthier salads with their main meals rather than fries. Benny's Burgers has also reduced the size of the portions of fries it serves to reduce its costs and to reduce the amount of fat and calories in its meal deals.

Sales revenue	£25,000,000
Gross profit	£9,000,000
Other operating expenses	£8,000,000

▲ **Table 1** Fried Fries plc's performance in 2023

Fixed costs	£25,000,000
Sales price per unit	£2.00
Variable cost per unit	£1.50

▲ **Table 2** Fried Fries plc's costs and sales price per unit of fries

10.1 Which *two* of the following are short-term sources of finance? **(2)**

  A Venture capital
  B Trade credit
  C Retained profit
  D Crowd funding
  E Overdraft

10.2 Explain *one* benefit to an entrepreneur of crowd funding. **(3)**

10.3 Explain *one* reason why paying overheads on time is important. **(3)**

10.4 Discuss the importance of venture capital to a start-up business. **(6)**

10.5 Define the term 'fixed cost'. **(1)**

10.6 Give one long-term source of finance that Fried Fries plc could utilise. **(1)**

> **EXAM TIP**
> When answering 'Calculate' questions, show your workings clearly. Marks will be awarded for correct elements, even if the final answer is incorrect.

10.7 Using the information in Table 1, calculate Fried Fries plc's cost of sales. You are advised to show your workings. **(2)**

> **EXAM TIP**
> Do not cross out any workings when answering 'Calculate' questions. Anything which is not crossed out can be marked. A correct answer that is crossed out will not be marked.

10.8 Using the data provided in Table 2, calculate Fried Fries plc's break-even point in units. You are advised to show your workings. **(2)**

10.9 Outline *one* disadvantage to Fried Fries plc of a rise in interest rates. **(2)**

> **EXAM TIP**
> You might want to revisit your answer to this question when you have revised flow production in Chapter 29.

10.10 Analyse the impact of increased use of technology in Fried Fries plc's factories. **(6)**

> **EXAM TIP**
> When answering 'Justify' questions, it is vital to plan your answer before you start writing. Often, students miss marks because their answers lack structure.

10.11 To ensure its long-term survival, Fried Fries plc is considering two options:
  Option 1: expanding the product range to include healthier alternatives
  Option 2: developing a new range of healthier baked fries.
  Justify which option Fried Fries plc should pursue. **(9)**

10.12 Evaluate the importance of accurate cash-flow forecasts for the success of Fried Fries plc. You should use the information provided as well as your knowledge of business. **(12)**

Knowledge

11 The options for start-up and small businesses

The concept of limited liability

Businesses owners choose whether they have **unlimited liability** or **limited liability**. Unlimited liability is riskier.

Unlimited liability	Limited liability
A business is **unincorporated**: it is not registered with the government, which means the business and its owners are the same in the eyes of the law.	A business is **incorporated**: it is registered with the government, which means the business and its owners are separated in the eyes of the law.
An unincorporated business has few legal requirements.	An incorporated business has legal requirements.
The owners are personally liable for the business's debts, and there is no limit to the financial loss an owner must personally cover. Business losses must be covered by the owners' personal assets (by the money and other valuable items they own).	The owners are not personally liable for the business's debts, and the amount of financial loss an owner must personally cover is limited to the money they have invested in the business. Personal assets do not need to be sold to cover business debts.
There is an increase in risk for owners, and potential investors and suppliers may have less confidence in the business because there is no continuity if the original owner dies.	There is a reduction in risk for owners, and potential investors and suppliers may have more confidence in the business because there is continuity if the owner dies.

The types of business ownership for start-ups

A legal structure must be chosen when a business is set up, and there are three main options:

- **sole traders** and **partnerships**, which are unincorporated
- **private limited companies**, which are incorporated.

Sole trader

One individual has full control of the business, and there are no other decision-makers. A sole trader may employ others, but employees do not make decisions about the business.

Advantages and disadvantages

- ✓ Cheap and easy to set up: if not employing others, the only legal requirement is to pay income tax to the government.
- ✓ Speed of decision-making and full control: decisions can be made quickly because there is just one decision maker, and profits are not divided.
- ✓ Privacy: financial documents are not shared publicly.

- ✗ Unlimited liability: sole traders risk losing personal assets.
- ✗ Limited sources of finance: sole traders may find it hard to get a loan and they cannot sell shares.
- ✗ Hard work: there are no other owners to share responsibility or tasks with.

Key terms Make sure you can write a definition for these key terms

franchise   franchisee   franchisor   incorporated   limited liability
partnership   private limited company   sole trader
training   unincorporated   unlimited liability

Partnership

Two or more people sign a legal document called a deed of partnership, in which they agree how they are going to run a business together and how profit will be shared.

Advantages and disadvantages

- ✓ Shared risk and decision-making: more partners mean more people to share losses and make decisions.
- ✓ Expertise: partners often have different and complementary skills.
- ✓ Privacy: financial documents are not shared publicly.

- ✗ Shared risk: disagreements and decisions made by partners legally impact all partners.
- ✗ Limited life of business: if one partner dies, the partnership comes to an end.
- ✗ Shared profits: any profits are divided between the partners.
- ✗ Unlimited liability: partners risk losing personal assets.

Private limited company

A private limited company is a business that is owned by shareholders. Shareholders must be approved by the person selling the shares, so they are often family, friends or trusted investors.

Advantages and disadvantages

- ✓ Limited liability: losses are limited to the amount invested.
- ✓ Easier to raise finance: finance can be raised by selling shares or getting a loan from a bank.
- ✓ Continued life of business: the business can continue even if the shareholders change.

- ✗ Shared profits: the profits are shared by the shareholders.
- ✗ Complexity: there is an annual legal burden: accounts have to be filed each year, and both a Memorandum of Association and Articles of Association are needed to register a limited company.
- ✗ Loss of privacy: financial information must be made public.

Starting up and running a franchise operation

Instead of setting up a new brand, an entrepreneur may choose to buy a **franchise**. A franchise is a business where the owner (the **franchisor**) allows an entrepreneur (the **franchisee**) to sell its goods and services using its brand name, in exchange for an initial fee and a share of profit.

> **REVISION TIP**
>
> Lots of very famous businesses are franchises, including McDonald's, Subway, and Swarovski. Research one to see what is needed to become a franchisee.

Running a franchise

Advantages and disadvantages

- ✓ Lower risk: franchisees purchase the right to use an established brand name, which customers are already aware of.
- ✓ Support: franchisors provide **training** and other support to ensure quality.
- ✓ National advertising: the franchisor runs national marketing campaigns to increase brand awareness.

- ✗ Strictly controlled: key decisions – such as the products sold, pricing, and staff uniforms – are made by the franchisor, and the franchisee has limited opportunities to make decisions.
- ✗ Shared reputation: the actions of the franchisor and other franchisees can affect the success of a franchisee's business.
- ✗ Cost: initial fees can be high, and profits must be shared with the franchisor.

Retrieval

Answer the questions below. Cover the answers column with a piece of paper and write down as many answers as you can. Check and repeat.

Questions | Answers

1. When the owners of a business are personally liable for a business's debts, do they have unlimited liability or limited liability?

Unlimited liability

2. 'The business and its owners are separated in the eyes of the law.' Does this statement describe an incorporated business or an unincorporated business?

An incorporated business

3. Give one disadvantage of being a sole trader.

One from: unlimited liability (sole traders risk losing personal assets) / limited sources of finance (sole traders may find it hard to get a loan and they cannot sell shares) / hard work (there are no other owners to share responsibility or tasks with)

4. State one advantage of a partnership.

One from: shared risk and decision-making (more partners mean more people to share losses and make decisions) / expertise (partners often have different and complementary skills) / privacy (financial documents are not shared publicly)

5. Identify one advantage of a private limited company.

One from: limited liability (losses limited to amount invested) / easier to raise finance (finance can be raised by selling shares or getting a loan from a bank) / continued life of business (the business can continue even if shareholders change)

6. What is a franchise?

A business where the owner (the franchisor) allows an entrepreneur (the franchisee) to sell its goods and services using its brand name, in exchange for an initial fee and a share of profit

Previous questions

Use the questions below to check your knowledge from previous chapters.

Questions | Answers

1. Why is it more difficult for an entrepreneur to create a cash-flow forecast?

Entrepreneurs are unlikely to have historical data they can use to predict cash outflows and cash inflows

2. Give one advantage of an overdraft.

One from: flexibility (only used when businesses do not have enough money available to pay bills) / speed (easy to arrange and available whenever needed)

Practice 11

Exam-style questions

11.1 Which *one* of the following describes a sole trader? (1)

    A Limited liability
    B Financial information is made public
    C Unlimited liability
    D Two or more people make decisions

11.2 Which *two* of the following describe a private limited company? (2)

    A Limited liability
    B Easier to raise finance
    C Unlimited liability
    D Profits are divided between partners
    E A brand name is purchased

11.3 Explain *one* advantage of an overdraft for a sole trader. (3)

11.4 Explain *one* reason why a deed of partnership is important for a new partnership business. (3)

11.5 Discuss the importance of limited liability to a start-up business. (6)

> Sally, a keen baker, started selling pre-packaged cake mixes at local food fairs. The small, home-based business was very successful. Sally created a social media fan page to promote 'Sally's Bakes' and to interact with customers.
>
> Recently, Sally has experienced a huge increase in orders direct from social media. She is concerned that she is no longer able to create the cake mixes in her house by herself. She wants to expand her business and grow quickly. She has calculated the amount of capital she will need to expand her business and it is significant.
>
> Sally currently operates as a sole trader, and is worried that she will not be able to fulfil all the orders herself even if she does rent kitchen facilities.

11.6 Outline *one* disadvantage to Sally of staying as a sole trader. (2)

11.7 Analyse the benefit to Sally of using a bank loan to expand her business. (6)

11.8 Analyse the impact on Sally of changing the business ownership to a private limited company. (6)

11.9 Evaluate whether Sally is likely to benefit from franchising her small business. You should use the information provided as well as your knowledge of the business. (12)

> **EXAM TIP**
>
> When asked to 'analyse the impact', state the impact, explain *how* the impact will affect the stakeholder, and then explain what the *consequence* of the impact will be. You must also ensure your answer contains specific reference to the case study.

Knowledge

12 Business location

Factors influencing business location

Businesses must choose the correct location to be successful. A specific location may be suitable for one business and unsuitable for another.

Decisions about where to locate a business are based on a number of factors, and businesses try to minimise costs and maximise revenue.

Proximity

The choice of location may depend on its proximity to the market, labour, materials and competitors.

Market

How important is it to be close to the customer? What is the demographic of the target customer segment? Will they travel?

- A convenient location increases **footfall** (the number of people passing a location within a given time period). However, a convenient location will probably be more expensive and will, therefore, require many regular customers for the business to be profitable.
- Customers are likely to travel to get exactly what they need from a specialist business, so a convenient location is less important. However, the number of customers is likely to be low, which means products must be high value for the business to be profitable.

> **REMEMBER**
> Demographic segmentation groups people by customer profiles or social and economic characteristics including age, gender, level of education, religion, family size, income or stage in life.

Labour

The labour required by the business is an important factor in location decisions.

- Are there enough workers living locally to meet the business's needs?
- If the business requires specialist skills, can the business attract employees with these skills to the location?
- How much will labour cost? Different areas of the country have different salary and wage demands; for example, people living in areas of high unemployment may accept lower pay.

Materials

Proximity to raw materials can be a factor influencing business location.

- Some businesses, such as mining or fishing, must be located close to raw materials.
- Bulk-reducing businesses (where the end product is smaller than the raw materials used to make it) and businesses with heavy raw materials often locate close to their suppliers to reduce costs.
- Bulk-gaining businesses (where the end product is bigger than the raw materials used to make it) often locate close to their customers, so good transport links are more important than proximity to raw materials.

Competitors

A business must decide whether to locate close to, or far away from, competitors to attract customers. Locating close to competition leads to:
- high competition, which means the customers are shared
- high footfall, because customers are attracted to areas of high competition.

Nature of the business activity

A business may choose a particular location because of the nature of its business activity, because it is easier to operate in that location. For example:

- **Retailers** with physical locations, such as a high street store or a village shop, and businesses that provide direct services, such as hairdressers and estate agents, tend to locate in busy and popular areas to maximise footfall.
- E-tailers that sell over the internet and businesses that provide indirect services, such as web designers, tend to locate somewhere cheaper with a good internet connection.
- Manufacturers often locate in cheaper areas with good transport links, and sometimes close to suppliers.

The impact of the internet on location decisions

The internet allows buyers and sellers to trade online.

E-commerce (using the internet to carry out business transactions) enables businesses to sell to customers 24 / 7, attract customers worldwide, and reduce the number of employees overall.

As a result:
- many businesses no longer need fixed premises: employees can work from home, reducing overheads
- businesses that do need fixed premises can choose a cheaper location, such as a business park, reducing overheads.

Key terms — Make sure you can write a definition for these key terms: e-commerce, footfall, retailer

Retrieval

Answer the questions below. Cover the answers column with a piece of paper and write down as many answers as you can. Check and repeat.

#	Questions	Answers
1	What do businesses try to do when making decisions about where to locate a business?	Minimise costs and maximise revenue
2	The choice of location may depend on its proximity to what four things?	Market; labour; materials; competition
3	A convenient location increases what?	Footfall
4	State one question a business must ask itself about labour when choosing a location.	One from: Are there enough workers living locally to meet the business's needs? / If the business requires specialist skills, can the business attract workers with these skills to the location? / How much will labour cost?
5	Identify one business that must be located close to raw materials.	One from: a mining business / a fishing business / or something similar
6	Locating close to competition leads to two things. What are they?	High competition (which means the customers are shared); high footfall (because customers are attracted to areas of high competition)
7	What does e-commerce enable businesses to do?	To sell to customers 24 / 7, attract customers worldwide, and reduce the number of employees overall
8	Give two ways the internet impacts on the decision about where to locate.	Many businesses no longer need fixed premises; businesses that do need fixed premises can choose a cheaper location

Previous questions

Use the questions below to check your knowledge from previous chapters.

#	Questions	Answers
1	What is the formula for net cash flow?	net cash flow = cash inflows − cash outflows in a given period
2	Give one disadvantage of being a sole trader.	One from: unlimited liability (sole traders risk losing personal assets) / limited sources of finance (sole traders may find it hard to get a loan and they cannot sell shares) / hard work (there are no other owners to share responsibility or tasks with)
3	Identify one advantage of a private limited company.	One from: limited liability (losses limited to amount invested) / easier to raise finance (finance can be raised by selling shares or getting a loan from a bank) / continued life of business (the business can continue even if shareholders change)

Practice 12

Exam-style questions

12.1 Which *one* of the following does not describe proximity to the market? **(1)**
  A Convenient location
  B Willingness of customer to travel
  C Customer demographics
  D The availability of labour

12.2 Which *two* of the following describe things a business thinks about when it is considering proximity to raw materials? **(2)**
  A Bulk reducing
  B High competition
  C Cost of labour
  D Bulk gaining
  E Footfall

12.3 Explain *one* aim a new business might have. **(3)**

12.4 Explain *one* disadvantage to a business of a location close to competitors. **(3)**

12.5 Discuss the importance of e-commerce to a start-up business. **(6)**

Ahmed has worked as a mechanic in a car dealership for many years. Many customers are shocked at how much it costs to get their cars serviced at the dealership. Ahmed has decided to set up as an independent mechanic, and believes that he can sell his services for much lower prices.

Ahmed has been researching available buildings that might be suitable for his new business. He needs a large space, with room to park cars while they wait to be serviced. He has identified two possible locations.

Location 1	Location 2
• Situated on a low-cost industrial estate out of town • Many existing competitors nearby • Large car park	• Situated in an expensive town-centre location, close to where people work • Few competitors nearby • Limited space for parking cars

---

12.6 Define the term 'service'. **(1)**

12.7 Outline *one* advantage to Ahmed of locating close to where his customers work. **(2)**

12.8 Analyse the impact on Ahmed of using personal savings to fund his new business. **(6)**

12.9 Ahmed must make a decision on which location to choose:
  Option 1: location 1
  Option 2: location 2.
  Justify which *one* of these two options Ahmed should choose. **(9)**

EXAM TIP

'Justify' questions require an extended answer that explains which one of the two options a business owner should choose. There is never a 'correct' answer: you must explain the pros and cons of your chosen option and why you have chosen it.

Knowledge

13 The marketing mix

What is the marketing mix?

The marketing mix is the key elements of a marketing plan: price, product, promotion and place work together to create a single message to attract customers.

The marketing mix

Price
Price is the amount a business charges its customers for a product. Factors influencing price include competition, the economy, and costs. Price, in turn, affects demand, revenue, and profit.

Product
Products are the goods and/or services that a business sells to its customers.

Promotion
Promotion is the activities a business carries out to raise awareness of its products and to encourage customers to make a purchase. Using a promotional model, such as AIDA (Awareness, Interest, Desire, Action), a business effectively increases visibility and sales of products.

Place
Place is how products are sold and distributed to customers.

13

How the elements of the marketing mix work together

The marketing mix is adapted to a product depending on how much money the business has to spend on marketing and a number of other factors.

Balancing the marketing mix based on the competitive environment

The marketing mix is affected by the number and power of the businesses competing in the same market. Businesses can balance the mix by:

- product: identifying a unique selling point (USP) to make its product stand out from the competition
- price: setting the price of its product in response to the competition, lowering the price to **undercut** competitors, or increasing the price to create a **premium brand**
- promotion: increasing the amount spent on promotion, to increase brand awareness and brand loyalty where there is little competition
- place: ensuring the place a product is sold is convenient for consumers and matches the brand's image.

The impact of changing consumer needs on the marketing mix

Effective market research helps a business understand the needs of consumers and adjust the marketing mix as consumer needs change. Consumer needs impact:

- product: businesses could consider adapting existing products or developing new products to keep up with consumer trends
- price: if consumers' disposable income changes, businesses could decide to adjust prices accordingly
- promotion: businesses could adapt promotional channels as technology changes, to make sure consumers see adverts on social media and web pages
- place: a business might develop its website and close some shops if consumers increasingly choose to shop online.

The impact of technology on the marketing mix

Technology changes the way customers browse, compare and buy products. It therefore has an impact on the marketing mix.

- product: new goods and services can be developed; for example, videos were replaced by DVDs, which, in turn, have been replaced by streaming services
- price: data can be used to adjust prices; for example, **dynamic pricing** sets prices based on real-time market demands
- promotion: social media enables businesses of all sizes to communicate directly with customers, and businesses can use **cookies** on their websites to build **customer profiles** so that advertising is targeted
- place: the rise of e-commerce means businesses do not necessarily need shops to sell to customers.

> **REVISION TIP**
>
> Organise group study sessions. You are more likely to revise and retain information if you work with another student, and explaining things to other people helps you develop important analytical skills.

Key terms — Make sure you can write a definition of these key terms:

cookies   customer profile   dynamic pricing   place   premium brand   price   undercut

Retrieval

Answer the questions below. Cover the answers column with a piece of paper and write down as many answers as you can. Check and repeat.

Questions / Answers

#	Question	Answer
1	What is the marketing mix?	The key elements of a marketing plan: price, product, promotion and place work together to create a single message to attract customers
2	What does price mean in the marketing mix?	The amount a business charges its customers for a product
3	What does product mean in the marketing mix?	Products are the goods and / or services that a business sells to its customers
4	What does place mean in the marketing mix?	How products are sold and distributed to customers
5	What does promotion mean in the marketing mix?	The activities a business carries out to raise awareness of its products and to encourage customers to make a purchase
6	The marketing mix is adapted to a product depending on how much money the business has to spend on marketing and a number of other factors. Name three of these factors.	Competitive environment; changing consumer needs; technology
7	Identify one impact of digital communication on the marketing mix.	One from: social media allows businesses of all sizes to communicate directly with customers / businesses can use cookies on their websites to build customer profiles so that advertising is targeted
8	Identify one impact of e-commerce on the marketing mix.	Businesses do not necessarily need shops to sell to customers

Previous questions

Use the questions below to check your knowledge from previous chapters.

#	Question	Answer
1	Identify one long-term source of finance that results in a business owner losing control over their business	One from: venture capital / share capital
2	State one question a business must ask itself about labour when choosing a location.	One from: Are there enough workers living locally to meet the business's needs? / If the business requires specialist skills, can the business attract workers with these skills to the location? / How much will labour cost?
3	What does e-commerce enable businesses to do?	To sell to customers 24/7, attract customers worldwide, and reduce the number of employees overall

13 The marketing mix

Practice 13

Exam-style questions

13.1 Which *one* of the following is not an element of the marketing mix? **(1)**
- **A** Price
- **B** Product
- **C** Place
- **D** Prestige

13.2 Which *two* of the following can affect the marketing mix? **(2)**
- **A** Tariffs
- **B** Type of business ownership
- **C** Social aims and objectives
- **D** Changing consumer needs
- **E** Competitive environment

13.3 Explain *one* reason why it is important for a business to understand the competitive environment. **(3)**

13.4 Explain *one* impact of technology on the pricing element of the marketing mix. **(3)**

13.5 Discuss the importance of place when setting up a new business. **(6)**

> Wooden Beds Ltd has been selling quality, handmade wooden bed frames for over 50 years. It has a website, but relies on customers visiting showrooms to place orders.
>
> Sales have been decreasing in recent years. Sales staff in showrooms have gathered feedback from potential customers about why they have not bought a bed frame. The main response is that the designs are old fashioned, and the bed frames are too expensive. Many customers now research and purchase bed frames online, and think Wooden Beds Ltd's website is poorly designed and inaccessible.

13.6 Outline *one* advantage to Wooden Beds Ltd of lowering the price of its bed frames. **(2)**

13.7 Analyse the impact of reviewing Wooden Beds Ltd's aims and objectives. **(6)**

13.8 Analyse the impact of effective market research on Wooden Beds Ltd's marketing mix. **(6)**

13.9 Evaluate the impact of the product on Wooden Beds Ltd's marketing mix. You should use the information provided as well as your knowledge of business. **(12)**

> **EXAM TIP**
>
> To successfully answer an 'Evaluate' question, you must show the extent of the impact on the business. The impact may be high or low, and will depend on evidence from the case study and your knowledge of business.

14 Business plans

The role and importance of a business plan

A **business plan** is a document for internal and external stakeholders. It is a guide that helps to ensure the success of a new business, and it should be written before the business is established.

Business plans should be clear and minimise the use of technical language. They should contain the following information:

The business idea
- A brief description of the products the business will sell
- The name, legal structure and experience of the entrepreneur

Business aims and objectives
- The long-term strategy of the business
- The SMART targets that the business will use to track progress in the short term
- Provides motivation and a sense of direction

Target market (market research)
- A summary of existing market research into the market, including competition, trends and consumer data, including the number of potential customers and key demographics
- An outline of future market research needed to develop a deeper understanding of the target market

Forecasts of costs, revenue, and profit
- Estimated cost of setting up the business and the day-to-day running costs
- Forecasted sales revenue and profit
- Used to create a budget

Cash-flow forecast
- A forecast of the amount of cash that will flow into and out of the business in a set time period (usually 12 months)
- Helps to identify and deal with periods of negative cash flow

Sources of finance
- The long-term sources of finance that will be used to set up the business
- The short-term sources of finance that will be used to maintain positive cash flow

Location
- Where the business will be situated
- Why the location chosen is suitable, including its proximity to the market, labour, materials, and competitors

Marketing mix
- An outline of how the 4Ps of the marketing mix will be used to attract customers
- Linked to business aims and objectives; target market (market research); costs, revenue, profit, and cash-flow forecasts

The purpose of planning business activity

Generally, writing a business plan helps an entrepreneur collect together all the relevant information in a logical manner, and it can be used as a tool to check progress as the business develops.

Specifically, a business plan helps an entrepreneur minimise risk and obtain finance.

Minimising risk
There are a lot of risks involved in setting up a new business: entrepreneurs can lose time and money if things don't work out. However, business plans help minimise these risks.
- Detailed planning identifies potential issues and helps an entrepreneur avoid them.
- Clear aims and objectives provide direction when making business decisions.
- Financial forecasts help an entrepreneur set budgets to monitor and control spending.

Obtaining finance
Entrepreneurs often need to raise long-term finance to start or grow a new business. Business plans help with this.
- Banks require a business plan before making a loan. They want to know how the money borrowed will be spent and how the business intends to repay the loan.
- Business plans help investors understand the business and its vision, as well as the long-term risk and potential return on their investment.

> **REVISION TIP**
> Take regular breaks. Learning in short bursts allows the brain to process and store information.

Key terms — Make sure you can write a definition for this key term: *business plan*

Retrieval

Answer the questions below. Cover the answers column with a piece of paper and write down as many answers as you can. Check and repeat.

Questions / Answers

#	Question	Answer
1	What is a business plan?	A document for internal and external stakeholders; a guide that helps to ensure the success of a new business
2	When should a business plan be written?	Before a business is established
3	Give three things a business plan should contain.	Three from: the business idea / business aims and objectives / target market (market research) / forecasts of costs, revenue, and profit / cash-flow forecast / sources of finance / location / marketing mix
4	Why is it important to include the business's aims and objectives in the business plan?	Because they provide motivation and a sense of direction
5	In a business plan, what are used to create budgets?	Forecasts of costs, revenue, and profit
6	In a business plan, what helps you to identify and deal with periods of negative cash flow?	Cash-flow forecast
7	What should the section of the business plan about sources of finance include?	Information about the long-term sources of finance that will be used to set up the business, and the short-term sources of finance that will be used to maintain positive cash flow
8	What is the general purpose of writing a business plan?	It helps an entrepreneur to collect together all the relevant information in a logical manner, and it can be used as a tool to check progress as the business develops
9	What is the specific purpose of a business plan?	It helps an entrepreneur minimise risk and obtain finance

Previous questions

Use the questions below to check your knowledge from previous chapters.

#	Question	Answer
1	What are two main reasons for requiring short-term sources of finance?	To cover the costs incurred during the production process, before products are sold; to cover unexpected costs or emergencies
2	What is the marketing mix?	The key elements of a marketing plan: price, product, promotion and place work together to create a single message to attract customers
3	Identify one impact of e-commerce on the marketing mix.	Businesses do not necessarily need shops to sell to customers

Practice 14

Exam-style questions

14.1 Which *one* of the following does a business plan help an entrepreneur do? **(1)**
- A Create an original business idea
- B Predict changes in technology
- C Obtain finance
- D Identify customer wants

14.2 Which *two* of the following is a business plan aimed at? **(2)**
- A Potential investors
- B Competitors
- C Future customers
- D The business owner
- E Suppliers

14.3 Explain *one* reason why a business might use long-term sources of finance. **(3)**

14.4 Explain *one* potential consequence of poor business planning. **(3)**

14.5 Discuss the importance of business planning for minimising risk when starting a new business. **(6)**

> Elias has ten years of experience managing cafes and fast-food restaurants. He has spotted an opportunity in his home town for locally-produced and competitively-priced home-cooked meals to cater to a growing tourist trade.
>
> Elias has identified an experienced chef to work in his new restaurant, but he does not have enough savings to buy all of the necessary kitchen equipment. He is considering applying for a bank loan, because the chef is unable to invest in the new business with him.

EXAM TIP

Highlight key information in the case study to use in your answers to Questions 14.6–14.9. Failing to use information from the case study will limit the number of marks you can be awarded.

14.6 Outline *one* advantage of Elias setting SMART targets. **(2)**

14.7 Analyse the impact on Elias of applying for a bank loan. **(6)**

14.8 Analyse the impact on Elias of understanding the target market. **(6)**

14.9 Evaluate the impact on Elias's potential new business of a well-researched business plan. You should use the information provided as well as your knowledge of business. **(12)**

Practice

Exam-style questions

Flowery Flowers is a florist. It sources its flowers from speciality suppliers in the UK and Europe. The business was founded in 2015 by John Rutland in Leeds and quickly gained a huge following because of John's expertise in marketing on social media.

Demand grew and John opened branches of Flowery Flowers in five more major cities in the UK to meet demand. He built strong relationships with international suppliers and is able to import the quantities of flowers he needs from Europe through the Port of Hull.

In 2020, to meet the growing demand and capitalise on Flowery Flowers' success, John decided to expand through franchising. He thought that the brand name, alongside centralised marketing and centralised purchasing of flowers, would be successful.

Franchising was a success. John soon sold the rights to 15 franchisees. Flowery Flowers now has its own website and ambitious plans for growth.

14.10 Give *one* element of the marketing mix. (1)

14.11 State *one* factor that influences Flowery Flowers' business location. (1)

14.12 Outline *one* factor that may have influenced John's decision to expand through franchising. (2)

14.13 Outline *one* benefit to Flowery Flowers of developing a business plan. (2)

14.14 Analyse the impact of an effective marketing mix on the Flowery Flowers brand. (6)

> **EXAM TIP**
> It is important to read the questions carefully. Here you are being asked to analyse the impact of an *effective* marketing mix, so the answer should be positive. An effective marketing mix will not have any negative elements, so you should not discuss potential problems in your answer.

14.15 A Flowery Flowers franchisee must pay for services provided by Flowery Flowers, including:
- monthly rent: £5000 + 2% of sales revenue
- fee to use stock ordering and management systems: 5% of sales revenue.

If a Flowery Flowers franchisee makes annual sales of £500,000, calculate:

(a) the annual rent paid to Flowery Flowers (2)

(b) the annual fee paid to use the stock ordering and management systems. (2)

You are advised to show your workings.

14.16 In order to improve the distribution of goods to its shops, Flowery Flowers is considering two options:

Option 1: invest in one large distribution centre close to the Port of Hull

Option 2: invest in a series of smaller regional hubs closer to the shops.

Justify which *one* of these two options Flowery Flowers should choose. (9)

14.17 Evaluate how changes in technology may impact the marketing mix for Flowery Flowers. You should use the information provided as well as your knowledge of business. (12)

> **EXAM TIP**
> When evaluating the impact that changes in technology may have on Flowery Flowers, it is important to consider the likely size of the impact: is it likely to be big or small?

Knowledge

15 Business stakeholders

Business stakeholders and their different objectives

There are many different stakeholders in business. Some have similar objectives, and some have competing objectives.

The importance of each stakeholder depends on the type of business, how it operates, and whether the stakeholder is internal (inside the business) or external (outside the business).

The objectives of internal stakeholders

Shareholders (owners)

Shareholders of private limited companies and public limited companies often want businesses to be profitable so that dividends are high and the value of their shares increases.

Sole traders and partnerships also want profits to be high to achieve their financial goals.

Other common objectives for owners include a positive reputation, growth in market share, and making the business attractive to investors.

Managers

Managers want to influence the direction of the business they work for: they want to minimise costs and increase profit to ensure the success of the business. In return, they hope to get good salaries, and experience job security and good working conditions.

Employees

Employees want to maximise their wages and job security, and improve their working conditions and opportunities for promotion and training.

The objectives of external stakeholders

Customers

Customers want the best possible product for the best possible price, with the best possible customer service.

Customers may also value things such as convenience (in the form of good parking perhaps), and clear and accurate product information.

Suppliers

Suppliers want to increase sales and profit, and they often do this by building long-term relationships with their customers.

Suppliers also want to be paid on time, and to communicate well with their customers.

Local community

Communities want to increase job opportunities in the local area, and reduce the environmental and social impacts of business activity. They may also want businesses to support local causes.

Pressure groups

Pressure groups are organisations that try to influence the behaviour of consumers, businesses, and governments. They normally have a specific ethical or environmental goal.

What pressure groups want will depend on whether they think the impact of business activity needs to be minimised (because of its negative impacts) or increased (because of its positive impacts).

The government

National, regional and local government want businesses to thrive to employ people and pay tax. National government passes legislation (laws), and national, regional and local government implement policies to protect workers, consumers, and the environment from harmful business activity.

15

Stakeholders and businesses

Businesses must try to maintain positive relationships with their stakeholders because positive relationships minimise conflict.

How stakeholders are affected by business activity

Positive effects
- ✅ Owners and shareholders: higher profit and higher dividends
- ✅ Managers and employees: secure jobs, with good pay and working conditions
- ✅ Customers: better products and more choice
- ✅ The government: more jobs and more tax paid

Negative effects
- ❌ Employees: if given unachievable targets and workloads increase
- ❌ Suppliers: if asked to reduce their prices
- ❌ Local community: increased noise, air and water pollution

REVISION TIP

When revising topics where different viewpoints compete, work with a partner. Choose two different viewpoints and discuss which is more important for making business decisions. This will help you develop your critical thinking.

How stakeholders impact business activity

Positive impacts
- ✅ Owners and shareholders: providing direction and enough finance to run the business well
- ✅ Managers and employees: working well together to meet the business's aims and objectives
- ✅ Suppliers: maintaining quality

Negative impacts
- ❌ Employees: if they decide to fight for better pay and working conditions
- ❌ Local community: if they create pressure groups to persuade the government to reduce the negative impacts of business activity
- ❌ The government: if they pass legislation to make businesses behave more responsibly

Possible conflicts between stakeholders

Shareholders, owners and managers want to increase **productivity** but …	… employees want to be paid more and have better working conditions.
	… the local community wants to reduce noise, air and water pollution.
Shareholders, owners and managers want to increase profitability but …	… customers want low-priced products.
	… the government wants to increase pay and living standards.
	… suppliers want to be paid fairly for the raw materials they provide.

Businesses must judge carefully the relative importance and power of each stakeholder, and make decisions that keep the most important stakeholders happy.

Key terms — Make sure you can write a definition for these key terms: productivity, pressure group

15 Knowledge

Retrieval

Answer the questions below. Cover the answers column with a piece of paper and write down as many answers as you can. Check and repeat.

Questions / Answers

#	Question	Answer
1	What does the importance of a stakeholder depend on?	The type of business, how it operates, and whether the stakeholder is internal or external
2	Identify one internal stakeholder.	One from: shareholders (owners) / managers / employees
3	Why do shareholders want businesses to be profitable?	So that dividends and the value of their shares increases
4	State one objective of employees.	One from: maximise wages / maximise job security / improve working conditions / improve opportunities for promotion and training
5	Identify one external stakeholder.	One from: customers / suppliers / local community / pressure groups / the government
6	Give one objective of a customer.	One from: best possible product / best possible price / best possible customer service / convenience / clear and accurate information
7	Suppliers want to increase sales and profit. How do they often do this?	By building long-term relationships with their customers
8	Identify the three levels of government.	National, regional and local
9	Why must businesses try to maintain positive relationships with their stakeholders?	Because positive relationships minimise conflict
10	Identify one stakeholder who may be negatively affected by business activity.	One from: employees / suppliers / local community

Previous questions

Use the questions below to check your knowledge from previous chapters.

#	Question	Answer
1	State one advantage of a partnership.	One from: shared risk and decision-making (more partners mean more people to share losses and make decisions) / expertise (partners often have different and complementary skills) / privacy (financial documents are not shared publicly)
2	What is a business plan?	A document for internal and external stakeholders; a guide that helps to ensure the success of a new business
3	What, in a business plan, helps to identify and deal with periods of negative cash flow?	Cash-flow forecast

15 Business stakeholders

Practice 15

Exam-style questions

15.1 Which *one* of the following is an internal stakeholder? **(1)**

- A Owner
- B Customer
- C Pressure group
- D Local community

15.2 Which *two* of the following are objectives of an employee? **(2)**

- A Good wages
- B Repeat custom
- C Job security
- D Best possible customer service
- E Increased dividends

15.3 Explain *one* benefit to a business of having a suitable marketing mix **(3)**

15.4 Explain *one* possible conflict that might arise between the owners of a business and the local community. **(3)**

15.5 Discuss why it is important for a business to maintain positive relationships with all of its stakeholders. **(6)**

> UK supermarket group, Food Favourites, has decided to cut costs to remain competitive. Staff costs and the cost of purchasing products to sell have increased because the UK government has increased the National Minimum Wage. Customers are also becoming more price sensitive because of a cost-of-living crisis.
>
> Food Favourites has cut the number of employees in the marketing department by half and has reduced the number of people on the shop floor by 30%. To increase efficiency, Food Favourites is increasing customer service training for all shop-floor employees.

15.6 Outline *one* advantage of reducing the number of employees at Food Favourites. **(2)**

15.7 Analyse how having fewer shop-floor employees might impact customers of Food Favourites. **(6)**

15.8 Analyse the impact on Food Favourites of increasing customer service training for all shop-floor staff. **(6)**

15.9 Evaluate the likely impact on Food Favourites of reducing the size of its marketing department. You should use the information provided as well as your knowledge of business. **(12)**

EXAM TIP

Remember to read each question carefully. If you are asked to write about the impact on customers, your answer should focus on the impact on customers, not the impact on employees or shareholders.

Knowledge

16 Technology and business

Types of technology used by business

Technology has a huge impact on the products we purchase, how we purchase them, and where they are purchased from.

The most common types of technology used by businesses are:

E-commerce

E-commerce is using the internet to carry out business operations. It:
- enables convenient, global, 24/7 trading
- requires constant and expensive technological updates
- requires search engine optimisation to improve a business's website so that customers can find it easily via a search engine.

Digital communications

Digital communications are the online tools people use to keep in touch and share information, and they include emails, Instagram, digital message boards, file-sharing tools, cloud storage, and video conferencing.
They enable:
- 24/7 communication
- people to work from anywhere, so businesses can consider reducing the size of their offices.

Social media

Social media is interactive technology that allows people to easily create and share content online. It allows:
- businesses to communicate constantly with potential and existing customers
- customers and pressure groups to influence businesses, because they are able to communicate their message to a lot of people quickly.

Payment systems

Payment systems are ways of settling financial transactions by transferring funds from one person or organisation to another. Technology has made it very easy for customers to pay for products efficiently, in one go or in instalments.
- E-commerce enables direct payments between bank accounts online in multiple currencies.
- Digital payment systems are quicker and cheaper than traditional payment systems.

Technology used by businesses

16

How technology influences business activity

Technology changes rapidly and it has a huge influence on business activity.

Sales

Sales can be made at any time, anywhere in the world, using any currency. This results in more customers and more sales.

Information about products can be easily shared with customers. This results in greater customer satisfaction, because customers know what is in stock and can make informed purchasing decisions.

Costs

Technology can lower costs. For example:
- It increases the speed and impact of communications, which can result in quicker decision-making.
- It automates processes such as record keeping and accounting, which can result in fewer employees.
- Marketing takes place via websites and social media, which is often cheaper than traditional print advertising.
- It enables video conferencing and digital communications, which can reduce travel time and speed up communication.

Marketing mix

Technology impacts all four elements of the marketing mix. For example:
- Product: it enables businesses to develop new products, which help businesses grow.
- Price: it enables dynamic pricing, which means prices change in response to real-time market demands and profit increases.
- Promotion: digital communications enable businesses of all sizes to communicate directly with customers, and cookies ensure advertising is targeted, resulting in reduced marketing costs and better customer profiles.
- Place: businesses no longer need shops to sell to customers, which reduces costs while providing customers with a convenient place to access products.

> **REVISION TIP**
>
> Choose a business that sells designer products to teenagers and a business that provides banking services, and look at how they communicate with their customers. Do they use similar or different methods? Why? Do they have the same types of customers?

16 Knowledge

Retrieval

Answer the questions below. Cover the answers column with a piece of paper and write down as many answers as you can. Check and repeat.

Questions / Answers

#	Question	Answer
1	What are the four most common types of technology used by businesses?	E-commerce; social media; digital communications; payment systems
2	Identify one feature of e-commerce.	One from: enables convenient, global, 24/7 trading / requires constant and expensive technological updates / requires search engine optimisation to improve a business's website so that customers can find it easily via a search engine such as Google or Bing
3	What does social media allow businesses to do?	Communicate constantly with potential and existing customers
4	What does social media allow customers and pressure groups to do?	To influence businesses, because they are able to communicate their message to a lot of people quickly
5	Which type of technology commonly used by businesses enables people to work from anywhere?	Digital communications
6	Are digital payment systems slower and more expensive than traditional payment systems?	No, they are quicker and cheaper
7	How does technology affect the price element of the marketing mix?	It enables dynamic pricing, which means prices change in response to real-time market demands and profit increases
8	How does technology affect the place element of the marketing mix?	Businesses no longer need shops to sell to customers, which reduces costs while providing customers with a convenient place to access products

Previous questions

Use the questions below to check your knowledge from previous chapters.

#	Question	Answer
1	Give three things a business plan should contain.	Three from: the business idea / business aim and objectives / target market (market research) / forecasts of costs, revenue and profit / cash-flow forecast / sources of finance / location / marketing mix
2	Identify one internal stakeholder.	One from: shareholders (owners) / managers / employees
3	Identify the three levels of government.	National, regional, and local

16 Technology and business

Practice 16

Exam-style questions

16.1 Which *one* of the following is a feature of e-commerce? **(1)**

  A Footfall
  B Face-to-face conversations
  C 24/7 trading
  D Cash payments

16.2 Which *two* of the following are features of digital communications? **(2)**

  A 24/7 communication
  B Face-to-face conversations
  C Direct payments between bank accounts
  D Automated processes
  E Some employees can work anywhere

16.3 Explain *one* benefit of using digital payment systems. **(3)**

16.4 Explain *one* way a business could balance the marketing mix. **(3)**

16.5 Discuss the impact on a business's costs of using technology. **(6)**

> Peace App Ltd produces apps for mobile devices. Its most successful app is 'Flower power', a mindfulness subscription service aimed at young professionals. It is very popular and sales have been strong. However, customers are starting to cancel their subscriptions and complaining on social media that the app is getting harder to use and the quality of the content is declining.
>
> Peace App Ltd has decided to cut costs and increase profit by closing its offices and asking all employees to work from home. It will rely on cloud storage and video conferencing. It already uses social media to promote its products to new customers.

16.6 Outline one advantage to Peace App Ltd of using digital communications. **(2)**

> **EXAM TIP**
> When answering an 'Outline' question, make sure that both points you make are linked together and refer to the case study.

16.7 Analyse the impact of falling cash inflows on Peace App Ltd. **(6)**

16.8 In order to increase the profitability of 'Flower power', Peace App Ltd is considering two options:

  Option 1: implementing a dynamic-pricing strategy

  Option 2: having regular, office-based team meetings.

  Justify which *one* of these two options Peace App Ltd should choose. **(9)**

16.9 Evaluate the likely impact of Peace App Ltd making its employees return to work in an office full time after two years of working at home. You should use the information provided as well as your knowledge of business. **(12)**

Knowledge

17 Legislation and business

Legislation

Parliament passes laws that businesses operating in the UK must follow.

- Consumer law is designed to protect consumers.
- Employment law is designed to protect employees.

The principles of consumer law

The Consumer Rights Act 2015 aims to ensure the quality of products consumers buy, and the rights of consumers when they purchase something.

Quality

Businesses must provide products that are:
- of reasonable quality (often determined by price)
- fit for their intended purpose
- as described to the customer.

Consumer rights

Customers have the right to:
- a full refund if an item is faulty, not as described, or does not do what it is supposed to do
- a full refund if they buy something online, by mail or over the phone within 14 days of receiving the goods even if they are not faulty
- the safe delivery of goods of the stated quality
- fair terms and conditions when entering a contract to purchase products.

The principles of employment law

Employment law protects employees by governing employees' rights at work, and the responsibilities employers have towards their employees.

There are four main areas of employment law.

1 Recruitment

Employers must ensure:
- a fair recruitment and selection policy
- employees receive a contract of employment, stating the key terms and conditions of employment
- they have checked an applicant is able to work in the UK.

2 Pay

Employment law regulates the minimum amount a person can be paid per hour by an employer. It usually increases every year.
- The National Living Wage is the minimum amount a person over 21 can be paid per hour.
- The **National Minimum Wage** is the minimum amount a person between the ages of 16 and 20, and an apprentice in the first year of an apprenticeship, can be paid per hour.

> **REMEMBER**
>
> An apprenticeship is a paid position that offers hands-on work experience while you work towards a qualification.

3 Discrimination

The Equality Act 2010 protects people from **discrimination** at work and in wider society. People are discriminated against when they are treated differently because of a protected characteristic.

4 Discrimination

The Health and Safety at Work Act 1974 highlights the importance of everyone in a workplace being responsible for the well-being of others.

The Act specifically requires employers to provide:
- safe working conditions
- suitable equipment and training if a role is dangerous
- compulsory health and safety training
- insurance against accidents in the workplace.

The impact of legislation on businesses

Businesses must keep up to date with new legislation and ensure their operations comply with all new laws. This can be costly, but there are positive consequences if businesses meet their legal obligations and serious negative consequences if they do not.

Costs can include:
- training employees
- providing specialist equipment
- meeting administrative requirements, including writing new policies and procedures, and updating manuals
- increasing wages, when minimum wage levels increase.

Positive consequences of meeting legal obligations	Negative consequences of not meeting legal obligations
✓ There is increased employee confidence and satisfaction. ✓ The business gains a reputation for being trustworthy, for its products and as an employer, which may attract customers and employees.	✗ Owners and employees may be prosecuted and punished with fines, and even prison sentences, for breaking the law. ✗ The business's reputation and brand may be damaged by negative publicity, which may reduce customer numbers and could eventually lead to a business closing.

REVISION TIP

To help you understand and remember what you are revising, try to find current, real-life examples of what you are studying in the news. Make notes on the Knowledge organiser to help you remember these examples.

Key terms — Make sure you can write a definition for these key terms: discrimination, National Minimum Wage

Retrieval

Answer the questions below. Cover the answers column with a piece of paper and write down as many answers as you can. Check and repeat.

	Questions	Answers
1	What passes laws that businesses operating in the UK must follow?	Parliament
2	Who is consumer law designed to protect?	Consumers
3	What are the aims of the Consumer Rights Act 2015?	To ensure the quality of products consumers buy, and the rights of consumers when they purchase something
4	When is a customer entitled to a full refund?	If an item is faulty, not as described, or does not do what it is supposed to do; if they buy something online, by mail or over the phone within 14 days of receiving goods even if they are not faulty
5	What are the four main areas of employment law?	Recruitment; pay; discrimination; health and safety
6	Give one thing employers need to ensure when recruiting.	One from: a fair recruitment and selection policy / employees receive a contract of employment, stating the key terms and conditions of employment / they have checked an applicant is able to work in the UK
7	Which law protects people from discrimination at work and in wider society?	The Equality Act 2010
8	What must a business provide if a role is dangerous?	Suitable equipment and training
9	State one negative consequence of not meeting legal obligations.	One from: owners and employees may be prosecuted and punished with fines, and even prison sentences, for breaking the law / the business's reputation and brand may be damaged by negative publicity, which may reduce customer numbers and could eventually lead to a business closing

Previous questions

Use the questions below to check your knowledge from previous chapters.

	Questions	Answers
1	What is the specific purpose of a business plan?	It helps an entrepreneur minimise risk and obtain finance
2	What are the four most common types of technology used by businesses?	E-commerce; social media; digital communications; payment systems
3	How does technology affect the price element of the marketing mix?	It enables dynamic pricing, which means prices change in response to real-time market demands and profit increases

17 Legislation and business

Practice 17

Exam-style questions

17.1 Which *one* of the following is covered by the Consumer Rights Act 2015? (1)

  A National Living Wage
  B Fair recruitment
  C Suitable equipment and training
  D Quality of products

17.2 Which *two* of the following requirements are covered by consumer law? (2)

  A Businesses must safely deliver goods of the stated quality
  B Employees should not be discriminated against
  C Products must be fit for their intended purpose
  D Businesses must provide compulsory health and safety training
  E Employees must receive a contract of employment

EXAM TIP

Look carefully at the number of marks available for each question. Try to spend, on average, one minute per mark when answering each question. The additional 15 minutes should be used to plan your longer answers. This will help you manage your time during your exams.

17.3 Explain *one* benefit to a business of complying with employment law. (3)

17.4 Explain *one* way a business owner could be affected by pressure groups. (3)

17.5 Discuss the impact on costs of complying with new legislation that applies to businesses. (6)

> Steel Rings plc makes metal pipes and valves in foundries across the UK. The foundries are dangerous places to work and require highly-skilled employees to manufacture the precision pipes and valves the business makes for industrial customers. Steel Rings plc takes training very seriously, and it has a number of apprentices who are training towards the specialist roles the business requires.
>
> The National Living Wage and the National Minimum Wage have recently increased, and new health and safety legislation has been passed. It requires all employees working in foundries to attend an annual training course run by an external provider.

17.6 Outline *one* advantage to Steel Ring plc of employing apprentices. (2)

17.7 Outline *one* drawback to Steel Rings plc of the new health and safety legislation. (2)

17.8 Analyse the impact on employees of Steel Rings plc of the annual health and safety training. (6)

17.9 Evaluate the likely impact on Steel Rings plc of the increase in the National Living Wage and the National Minimum Wage. You should use the information provided as well as your knowledge of business. (12)

Knowledge

18 The economy and business

The impact of the economic climate on business

The national economy of a country influences business activity. The major economic impacts include:

- the cost of and availability of labour
- the cost of, and ease of access to, borrowing
- the amount of money customers have to spend on purchases.

If the national economy is strong:
- ✓ the economy grows
- ✓ wages and salaries may increase
- ✓ customers are more likely to spend than save.

If the national economy is weak:
- ✗ the economy contracts and can go into **recession** (a period of economic decline that lasts longer than six months)
- ✗ wages and salaries may decrease
- ✗ customers are more likely to save than spend.

Aspects of the economic climate and their impact on business

There are many aspects of a national economy that can influence business activity.

Unemployment

The government measures the number of people who are employed (who are working) and the number of people who are actively seeking work (who are willing and able to work but are unemployed).

If employment is high and unemployment is low:
- there are fewer potential employees for businesses to hire, which can slow business growth plans
- wages and salaries often increase because businesses compete for employees, which can increase wage and salary costs.

If employment is low and unemployment is high:
- there are likely to be fewer potential customers for **luxury goods**, which can cause businesses to change their aim from profit to survival
- wages and salaries often decrease because there is more competition for jobs, which reduces the amount of money available for luxury goods.

Changing levels of consumer income

Levels of consumer income are often affected by levels of employment.

An increase in consumer income leads to higher disposable income.

↓

This means consumers are more likely to buy luxury goods, and businesses are more likely to invest to meet increased demand and expand their product range.

↓

A decrease in consumer income leads to lower disposable income.

↓

This means consumers are more likely to buy budget ranges and save their cash for emergencies. This can reduce demand, and cause businesses to cut costs.

Key terms — Make sure you can write a definition for these key terms: cost of living, exchange rate, export, import, inflation, interest rate, luxury goods, recession

Inflation

Inflation is the rate at which prices increase over a period of time.

- Increases in costs can cause businesses to increase the price of their products.
  ↓
- Inflation rises.
  ↓
- This causes the **cost of living** (the amount of money a person needs to spend to pay for essentials) to increase.
  ↓
- As a result, employees demand pay rises to allow them to maintain their standard of living.

- Demand for products decreases and/or businesses find it hard to access short- and long-term sources of finance.
  ↓
- Businesses respond by lowering their prices to encourage customers to buy their products.
  ↓
- Inflation decreases.
  ↓
- The economy can contract and go into recession. If this happens, some businesses will close and unemployment is likely to increase.

Changes in interest rates

Banks and other organisations pay interest on savings and charge interest on loans and overdrafts. The amount of interest payable depends on the **interest rate**.

Interest is a percentage of the money saved or loaned. The interest rate can vary depending on the level of risk involved, and how long the money is being saved or borrowed for.

If interest rates rise:
- the cost of borrowing increases
- consumer demand decreases
- businesses tend to reduce investment to avoid future cash-flow problems
- savings increase.

If interest rates fall:
- the cost of borrowing decreases
- consumer demand increases
- businesses tend to increase investment as the cost of capital investment decreases
- economic growth occurs.

Government taxation

The government taxes business activity, and uses the money raised to fund public services. Taxes affecting businesses include:

- VAT (value added tax) is a tax that businesses with a sales revenue over a certain amount have to charge their customers. If the government lowers VAT, products may become cheaper, and consumer demand may increase. If the government increases VAT, products may become more expensive, and consumer demand may decrease.

- Income tax is a tax paid by individuals on the money they earn. If income tax is lowered, disposable income increases, and consumer demand may increase. If income tax is increased, disposable income decreases, and consumer demand may decrease.
- Corporation tax is paid by businesses on their profits. If corporation tax is lowered, retained profit can increase, and businesses may spend more on expanding. If corporation tax is increased, retained profit may decrease, and businesses may spend less on expanding.

Changes in exchange rates

The **exchange rate** is the value of one country's currency in relation to another; for example, £1 is equal to US$1.32. Exchange rates change constantly.

Exchange rates are very important to businesses that **import** raw materials, or import or **export** products to another country, but changing exchange rates affect all businesses in some way.

Two acronyms can help you remember the impact of exchange rates on businesses:

SPICED: Strong Pound, Imports Cheaper, Exports Dearer

WPIDEC: Weak Pound, Imports Dearer, Exports Cheaper

Retrieval

Answer the questions below. Cover the answers column with a piece of paper and write down as many answers as you can. Check and repeat.

Questions | Answers

#	Question	Answer
1	Identify one major economic impact on business activity of changes in the national economy.	One from: the cost of and availability of labour / the cost of, and ease of access to, borrowing / the amount of money customers have to spend on purchases
2	What happens if the economic impacts are positive?	The economy grows; wages and salaries increase; customers are more likely to spend than save
3	Identify one impact of low unemployment levels.	One from: there are fewer potential employees for businesses to hire, which can slow business growth plans / wages and salaries often increase because businesses compete for employees, which can increase wage and salary costs
4	What does it mean for businesses when an increase in consumer income leads to higher disposable income?	It means consumers are more likely to buy luxury goods, and businesses are more likely to invest to meet increased demand and expand their product range
5	What does it mean for businesses when a decrease in consumer income leads to lower disposable income?	It means consumers are more likely to buy budget ranges and save their cash for emergencies, which can reduce demand and cause businesses to cut costs
6	What happens when inflation rises?	The cost of living increases and, as a result, employees demand pay rises to allow them to maintain their standard of living
7	Identify one tax that affects businesses.	One from: VAT / income tax / corporation tax
8	The acronyms SPICED and WPIDEC help us remember the effects of exchanges rates on business. What do they stand for?	SPICED: Strong Pound, Imports Cheaper, Exports Dearer; WPIDEC: Weak Pound, Imports Dearer, Exports Cheaper

Previous questions

Use the questions below to check your knowledge from previous chapters.

#	Question	Answer
1	Which type of technology commonly used by businesses enables people to work from anywhere?	Digital communications
2	What are the aims of the Consumer Rights Act 2015?	To ensure the quality of products consumers buy, and the rights of consumers when they purchase something
3	What must a business provide if a role is dangerous?	Suitable equipment and training

Practice 18

Exam-style questions

18.1 Which *one* of the following is *not* a sign that all is well with a country's economy? **(1)**

- A Economic growth
- B Increased wages
- C A recession
- D Increased consumer spending

> **EXAM TIP**
> If you are unsure of the correct answer to a multiple-choice question, first try to remove answer options you know are incorrect.

18.2 Which *two* of the following are benefits to businesses of an increase in consumer income? **(2)**

- A Increase in people saving
- B Higher disposable incomes
- C Reduction in demand for luxury goods
- D Growth in demand for luxury goods
- E Growth in demand for budget ranges

18.3 Explain *one* source of finance for capital investment. **(3)**

18.4 Explain *one* way a business owner could be affected by high interest rates. **(3)**

18.5 Discuss the impact on businesses of changing exchange rates. **(6)**

The Jewel Company plc imports diamonds from international suppliers and sells them to the public through a network of luxury jewellers in cities in the UK. The target customer has a high level of disposable income, and the size of the diamond often matters more than the price.

In recent years, synthetic diamonds have become much more popular. They are larger and less than half the price of natural diamonds. The UK is in a period of recession and the value of the pound is very low. As a result, wealthy customers are becoming more price conscious and are increasingly buying synthetic diamonds.

> **EXAM TIP**
> It is important to Interpret and use data effectively to support, inform and justify business decisions. Make sure that you read the case study carefully and think through likely effects of the information provided and how it can help you answer the exam questions.

18.6 Outline *one* advantage to The Jewel Company plc of consumers having high levels of disposable income. **(2)**

18.7 Outline *one* disadvantage to The Jewel Company Plc of the UK being in a period of recession. **(2)**

18.8 Analyse the impact on The Jewel Company plc of a rise in corporation tax. **(6)**

18.9 Evaluate the likely impact on The Jewel Company plc of a weak pound. You should use the information provided as well as your knowledge of business. **(12)**

Knowledge

19 External influences

The importance of external influences on business

There are many external influences that businesses cannot control, including technology, legislation and the economic climate. These influences can present an opportunity to gain a **competitive advantage** or a threat that can stop a business achieving its goals.

Businesses must be able to react and adapt to external influences if they are to survive and grow. If they do not, their brand can be damaged, they can lose market share, or they can fail.

Possible responses by businesses to changes in technology

Technology often changes gradually, but sometimes significant changes happen very quickly. This can make it difficult for businesses to decide when to invest in responding to technological changes.

If a business is too slow to innovate:

- the goods and services it sells can become obsolete
- competitors can become more efficient or attract customers away
- the business can damage its brand image and lose market share.

However, if a business waits to innovate, it can charge lower prices for its products because its costs are lower than its competitors' costs.

Possible responses by businesses to changes in legislation

Legislation changes regularly, and businesses must comply with legislation even if doing so adds to their costs.

The consequences of not complying are serious and include fines, imprisonment, and loss of reputation. Businesses can also be forced to close.

Possible responses by businesses to changes in the economic climate

Businesses must carry out market research continuously to understand how they are being impacted by changes in the economic climate.

Here are some examples of how changes in the economic climate can affect a business:

Changes can be positive	Changes can be negative
• A rise in consumer income can increase demand, which can lead to new product development. • Taxation falls, which leads to price reductions, which can increase demand. • Interest rates fall, which can lead to an increase in borrowing and investment.	• Falling exchange rates can lead to a weak pound, making imports more expensive and causing price rises. • Inflation increases, which can reduce consumers' disposable income and reduce profit. • Unemployment increases, which can lower demand and force price reductions as businesses compete for customers.

Key terms — Make sure you can write a definition for this key term: competitive advantage

Retrieval 19

Answer the questions below. Cover the answers column with a piece of paper and write down as many answers as you can. Check and repeat.

Questions | Answers

1. Give three external influences that affect businesses. | Technology; legislation; the economic climate

2. Why must businesses be able to react and adapt to external influences? | To survive and grow

3. Identify one thing that can happen if a business is too slow to innovate in response to technological changes. | One from: the goods and services it sells can become obsolete / competitors can become more efficient or attract customers away / the business can damage its brand image and lose market share

4. Give one consequence of not complying with legislation. | One from: fines / imprisonment / loss of reputation / forced to close

5. What can happen if interest rates fall? | It can lead to an increase in borrowing and investment by businesses

Previous questions

Use the questions below to check your knowledge from previous chapters.

Questions | Answers

1. What does social media allow businesses to do? | Communicate constantly with potential and existing customers

2. Identify one tax that affects businesses. | One from: VAT / income tax / corporation tax

Practice

Exam-style questions

19.1 Explain *one* way in which new technology is a cost to a business. (3)

19.2 Explain *one* way a business could be affected by changes in the economic climate. (3)

19.3 Discuss the impact on businesses of a rapidly changing economic climate. (6)

Practice

Exam-style questions

Retirement Homes Ltd provides long-term care to senior citizens who are no longer able to look after their own health and well-being effectively. It owns two retirement brands that operate throughout the UK, each targeting different market segments. El Basico targets people whose fees are paid by the state, and Casa De Luxe targets wealthier people who pay for their own care. In 2024, the average cost per week of a room at Casa De Luxe was £1000.

Since 2023, the economic climate has been poor. Inflation and interest rates are high. Retirement Homes Ltd is still paying off the significant, long-term borrowing it took out to purchase the care homes, and it makes a profit by paying its employees the National Living Wage and providing them with the minimum possible training required by law.

In 2024, the government increased the National Living Wage to £12.50 per hour, in line with inflation. In addition to this, a new competitor, Mid-Range Retirement Ltd has reduced Casa De Luxe's market share. Mid-Range Retirement Ltd care homes use the latest technology to care for residents, which is a major attraction to senior citizens who are increasingly used to technology.

19.4 Define the term 'brand'. (1)

19.5 State *one* benefit to Retirement Homes Ltd of changes in technology. (1)

19.6 Outline *one* way in which Retirement Homes Ltd segments the market. (2)

19.7 Outline *one* benefit to Retirement Homes Ltd of high unemployment levels. (2)

19.8 Analyse the impact of changing levels of consumer income on the Casa De Luxe brand. (6)

19.9 Using the information provided, calculate the annual cost of a room at Casa De Luxe in 2024. You are advised to show your workings. (2)

19.10 To add value to its Casa De Luxe brand, Retirement Homes Ltd is considering two options:

Option 1: raise capital to invest in upgrading obsolete technology

Option 2: review the marketing mix to attract more customers.

Justify which *one* of these two options Retirement Homes Ltd should choose. (9)

> **EXAM TIP**
> When answering a 'Justify' question, link each option to relevant chapters in this revision guide. For example, Option 1 relates to Chapters 1 and 10 (business dynamics and finance), while Option 2 could refer to Chapters 6 and 13 (competition and the marketing mix). Choose the option that is more relevant to the business's aims and objectives.

19.11 Evaluate the impact changes in employment law may have on Retirement Homes Ltd. You should use the information provided as well as your knowledge of business. (12)

Knowledge

20 Business growth

Methods of business growth

As a business becomes established it is likely to set growth as one of its objectives. There are two methods of business growth: **internal (organic) growth** and **external (inorganic) growth**.

Internal (organic) growth

A business can grow from the inside by increasing its trading activities. This can be done by developing new goods and services or by entering new markets.

New goods and services	New markets
New goods and services can be developed through: - innovation: new goods and services are designed and launched into the market - research and development: new goods and services are developed through scientific research and technological development.	Business can enter new markets by: - changing the marketing mix to attract new customers; for example, adding a new product line - taking advantage of technology to increase the number of customers; for example, using e-commerce to reach new customers - expanding overseas; for example, launching a product in Asia.

Internal (organic) growth
Advantages and disadvantages

✓ Brand is not damaged: not diluted by a merger or compromised by a takeover	✗ Likely to be slower than external growth
✓ Less expensive than external growth	✗ Unlike external growth, no opportunity to gain expertise from another business
✓ Plays to existing strengths	✗ May take a long time to recover costs

Key terms — Make sure you can write a definition for these key terms

equity   external (inorganic) growth   external sources of finance   internal (organic) growth   internal sources of finance   loan capital   merger   public limited company (plc)   stock market flotation   takeover

External (inorganic) growth

A business can grow from the outside by joining with other businesses. This can be done through **mergers** or **takeovers**.

Mergers	Takeovers
Two or more businesses agree to join together to operate as one. They share resources and expertise, and thereby reduce costs.	One business buys a second business. The two companies may begin trading under one name, or the two businesses can continue trading under two separate names. Takeovers can be hostile (the business is bought reluctantly) or friendly (the business agrees to be bought).

External (inorganic) growth
Advantages and disadvantages

- ✓ Can quickly gain market share
- ✓ Can quickly add new products and/or markets to the business
- ✓ Can gain expertise
- ✓ Can lower costs in the long term
- ✗ Expensive to buy another business
- ✗ May be a conflict of interest between the two businesses
- ✗ May damage a brand's reputation if, for example, the business's operations change and there is a fall in quality

Types of business growth for growing businesses

As a business grows, it may look to change the way it is owned, changing from a private limited company to a **public limited company (plc)**. One of the main reasons for doing this is to raise additional finance to fund growth.

Public limited company (plc)

A public limited company (plc) is a business that can sell shares to the public on a stock market, and has limited liability. It is owned by its shareholders; each shareholder is a part owner of the business.

Advantages and disadvantages

- ✓ Able to raise finance by selling shares on a stock market
- ✓ Limited liability
- ✓ Greater power when negotiating with other organisations, such as suppliers and banks, because of its size
- ✓ Seen as more reliable than other forms of ownership because customers perceive it as an established business
- ✗ Complex to set up
- ✗ Greater legal requirements in terms of accounting and reporting
- ✗ Records are available for everyone to see, including competitors
- ✗ Risk of a hostile takeover

> **LINK**
> It is important to understand what is meant by limited liability and why this may be seen as an advantage. Revisit the concept of limited liability covered in Chapter 11.

Knowledge

20 Business growth

Sources of finance for growing and established businesses

As a business grows, it requires finance to pay for this growth; for example, it requires finance to pay for research and development or to take over another business. Because the business is now growing or established, it has access to additional sources of finance both from within the business and from external sources.

> **LINK**
>
> Look back at Chapter 10 to remind yourself of the sources of finance available to start-ups or established small businesses. A growing or established business has access to additional sources of finance, which are discussed in this chapter.

Internal sources of finance

Internal sources of finance come from within a business, and they include retained profit and selling assets.

Retained profit

Retained profit is profit from previous years, and it can be used to fund growth.

Advantages and disadvantages

✓ Does not have to be repaid	✗ The amount available may be limited
✓ No interest charged	✗ May upset shareholders if the profit is retained to fund growth and not used to pay dividends
✓ No complex application procedures	
✓ No partial loss of ownership because **equity** is not given to shareholders	

Selling assets

A business can sell assets, such as machinery or land, to receive an immediate lump sum cash inflow that can be used to fund growth.

Advantages and disadvantages

✓ Does not have to be repaid	✗ Value of the assets may be low
✓ No interest charged	✗ Can be expensive in the long run if the assets are still needed
✓ Can dispose of unwanted assets	

External sources of finance

External sources of finance come from outside a business, and include **loan capital** and share capital.

Loan capital

Loan capital is finance borrowed from a bank or other financial organisations that must be repaid, with interest, over a pre-agreed period of time.

Advantages and disadvantages

- ✓ Paid back in regular instalments so easy to budget for the repayments
- ✓ Relatively easy to apply for, because banks normally have online application forms

- ✗ The amount borrowed must be repaid, unlike share capital
- ✗ Interest is charged on the loan and may increase over the course of the loan
- ✗ Repayments and interest payments have to be paid regardless of whether the business has made a profit or not
- ✗ May have to be secured against an asset, such as premises. This means that, if repayments are not made, the bank can take ownership of the asset

Share capital

Share capital is finance raised from the sale of shares on a stock market, and it can be used to fund growth. Individuals or businesses buy shares in return for equity in the business, which means they are partial owners of the business and they receive a share of the business's profits in the form of dividends.

Advantages and disadvantages

- ✓ Does not need to be repaid
- ✓ Large sums of finance can be raised
- ✓ The business can decide when to make dividend payments and how much they will be.

- ✗ Partial loss of ownership as shareholders are part owners of the business
- ✗ Shareholders may expect dividends
- ✗ Risk of takeover, because another business may be able to buy 51% of the shares and will have the majority vote when major decisions are made
- ✗ Stock market flotation is a complex process

> **REMEMBER**
>
> A **stock market flotation** is the process a company goes through to become a public limited company. The business makes shares available on a stock market. This allows it to raise finance from the sale of shares to the general public and to other businesses.

> **REVISION TIP**
>
> Theme 2 is about a growing business. Think about this as you revise the content to consider how each point relates to a business with an objective of growth.

Retrieval

Answer the questions below. Cover the answers column with a piece of paper and write down as many answers as you can. Check and repeat.

	Questions	Answers
1	What is meant by internal growth?	A business grows from the inside by increasing its trading activities
2	What is another name for internal growth? Is it organic growth or inorganic growth?	Organic growth
3	List two ways of achieving internal growth.	Developing new goods and services; entering new markets
4	State one advantage of internal growth.	One from: the brand is not damaged: it is not diluted by a merger or compromised by a takeover / less expensive than external growth / plays to existing strengths
5	What is meant by external growth?	A business grows from the outside by joining with other businesses
6	State one advantage of external growth.	One from: can quickly gain market share / can quickly add new products and / or markets to the business / can gain expertise / can lower the costs in the long term
7	What is a public limited company?	A business that can sell shares on a stock market, and has limited liability
8	List two internal sources of finance.	Retained profit; selling assets
9	Distinguish between loan capital and share capital.	Loan capital is finance borrowed from a bank or other financial organisations. Share capital is finance raised by selling shares on a stock market
10	What is a stock market flotation?	The process a company goes through to become a public limited company, and makes shares available on a stock market

Previous questions

Use the questions below to check your knowledge from previous chapters.

	Questions	Answers
1	'The business and its owners are separated in the eyes of the law.' Does this statement describe an incorporated business or an unincorporated business?	An incorporated business
2	Give three external influences that affect businesses.	Technology; legislation; the economic climate
3	What can happen if interest rates fall?	It can lead to an increase in borrowing and investment by businesses

Practice 20

Exam-style questions

20.1 Which *one* of the following is an internal source of finance? **(1)**

A Loan capital C Retained profit
B Share capital D Stock market flotation

EXAM TIP

You will be awarded one mark for identifying an advantage and up to two additional marks for explaining why it is an advantage. For example, if you choose 'can quickly gain market share' as your advantage, you could explain how this occurs: because the market share of the businesses coming together is added together, which results in a bigger market share for the combined business.

20.2 Which *two* of the following are methods of inorganic growth? **(2)**

A Merger D Expanding overseas
B New products E Takeover
C New markets

20.3 Explain *one* advantage of external (inorganic) growth to a business. **(3)**

20.4 Explain *one* disadvantage of internal (organic) growth to a business. **(3)**

20.5 Discuss the impact on a business of selling assets to raise finance. **(6)**

EXAM TIP

The impact on a business is the advantages and disadvantages to the business of doing something.

> Greetings plc is a UK company that sells greeting cards, gift wrap and small gifts. It has 250 shops at train stations and airports.
>
> Greetings plc plans to open an additional 25 shops next year. The new shops will be located in city centres popular with tourists, such as York and Oxford. This growth will be financed using loan capital.

20.6 State *one* internal source of finance Greetings plc could use to fund growth. **(1)**

20.7 Outline *one* drawback to Greetings plc of being a public limited company. **(2)**

20.8 Analyse the impact on Greetings plc of using loan capital as a source of finance for growth. **(6)**

20.9 Evaluate whether internal (organic) growth will enable Greetings plc to increase its profits. You should use the information provided as well as your knowledge of business. **(12)**

Knowledge

21 Changes in business aims and objectives

Business aims and objectives

Business aims and objectives are the goals and targets a business sets for itself. As a business evolves, its aims and objectives change. For example, a start-up business is likely to focus on survival, whereas an established business may focus on growth.

LINK

Look back at Chapter 7 to remind yourself what business aims and objectives are, and the common aims and objectives of start-up businesses.

Why do business aims and objectives change as businesses evolve?

A business's aims and objectives change as businesses evolve in response to external and internal factors.

External factors

External factors are factors outside the control of businesses, such as **market conditions**, technology, and legislation.

Market conditions

Market conditions are the factors that determine the external environment in which a business operates.

The number of businesses competing in the same market can change. For example:
- new businesses enter the market
- existing businesses exit the market.

The state of the economy can change. For example:
- consumers have more or less disposable income to spend
- interest rates rise or fall, affecting the cost of loans to individuals and businesses
- inflation rises or falls, affecting prices
- exchange rates change, affecting the cost of importing raw materials or the price at which products can be sold abroad.

Technology

Advances in technology present businesses with new opportunities. For example:
- new e-commerce opportunities emerge
- new technology presents opportunities to change processes to increase efficiency
- technology makes entering international markets a possibility for the first time.

Legislation

New legislation can change how a business must operate. For example:
- an increase in the National Living Wage means businesses may need to review their profit margins
- new health and safety legislation means businesses may need to review their processes
- a ban on zero-hours contracts means businesses may need to review how they set employee hours.

LINK

In Chapter 18, you revised the economy and business. When revising why business aims and objectives change in relation to market conditions, go back and revise aspects of a national economy such as inflation and interest rates. Consider how business aims and objectives might change in response to changes in these aspects.

Internal factors

Internal factors are factors inside the control of the businesses.

They include:
- change of ownership
- change of leadership
- financial performance
- personal objectives of managers and employees
- change in **organisational structure**.

How do business aims and objectives change?

Aims and objectives change as businesses make decisions in response to external and internal factors.

Focus on survival or growth

For example, changes in market conditions or in the economic climate may mean a business can change its aims and objectives from survival to growth or vice versa.

Entering or exiting markets

For example, a new leader may have a different view of what the business should be focussing on, and the aims and objectives could change. They might close stores and take the business entirely online, or they might open stores in new international markets.

Growing or reducing the workforce

For example, technological advancements may mean a business changes its aims and objectives to increase the use of machinery and reduce the size of the workforce.

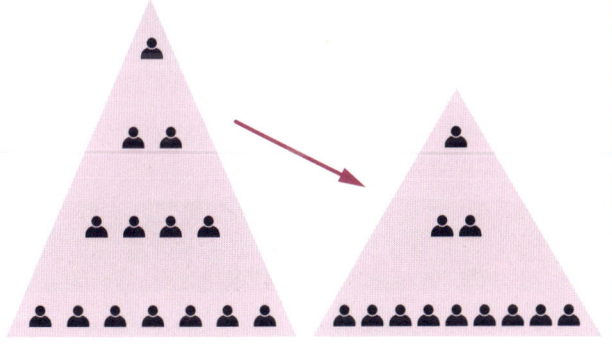

Increasing or decreasing product ranges

For example, a downturn in the economy may mean a business introduces a value range that is more affordable to its customers, or it might reduce the number of lines it sells in its shops.

Key terms — Make sure you can write a definition for these key terms: market conditions, organisational structure

Retrieval

Answer the questions below. Cover the answers column with a piece of paper and write down as many answers as you can. Check and repeat.

Questions / Answers

#	Question	Answer
1	What are business aims and objectives?	The goals and targets a business sets for itself
2	Give three external reasons why business aims and objectives change as businesses evolve.	Market conditions; technology; legislation
3	Give two examples of changes to the state of the economy that can cause a business to change its aims and objectives.	Two from: consumers have more or less disposable income to spend / interest rates rise or fall, affecting the cost of loans to individuals and businesses / inflation rises or falls, affecting prices / exchange rates change, affecting the cost of importing raw materials or the price at which products can be sold abroad
4	Give one example of how advances in technology can present businesses with new opportunities.	One from: new e-commerce opportunities emerge / new technology presents opportunities to change processes to increase efficiency / technology makes entering international markets a possibility for the first time
5	Give two internal reasons why business aims and objectives change as businesses evolve.	Two from: change of ownership / change of leadership / financial performance / personal objectives of managers and employees / change in organisational structure
6	How might a new leader result in a business's aims and objectives changing?	A new leader may have a different view of what the business should be focussing on, and the aims and objectives could change from achieving growth in the home market to expanding into new international markets
7	If a business changes its aims and objectives to increase the use of machinery, what might happen to the size of the workforce?	The size of the workforce may be reduced

Previous questions

Use the questions below to check your knowledge from previous chapters.

#	Question	Answer
1	What is meant by internal growth?	A business grows from the inside by increasing its trading activities
2	List two ways of achieving internal growth.	Developing new goods and services; entering new markets
3	What is meant by external growth?	A business grows from the outside by joining with other businesses

21 Changes in business aims and objectives

Practice 21

Exam-style questions

21.1 Which *one* of the following is an internal reason why business aims and objectives change as a business evolves? **(1)**

- **A** Change of leadership
- **B** Stricter health and safety legislation
- **C** New competitors
- **D** Advances in technology

21.2 Explain *one* way in which a business's aims and objectives may change as the business evolves. **(3)**

21.3 Discuss the impact of changing market conditions on a business's aims and objectives. **(6)**

Shiaz started in 2012 as a small-scale manufacturer of Indian ready meals. These were mainly sold through independent food retailers in Bradford, where the company was based. In 2017, Shiaz invested heavily in growth, bringing out ranges of sauces, breads, and vegan baby foods. As a result, it won a contract with a major supermarket chain.

Manisha, Shiaz's managing director, had an aim of growth. However, recently, things have not gone as well as she had hoped. The price of ingredients has risen, so costs are rising rapidly. In addition, some of the ingredients imported from Spain are in short supply because lower-than-expected rainfall for several years has affected Spanish crops.

In 2024, Shiaz failed to make a profit and was forced to reduce the size of its workforce. At a meeting, the board of directors voted to halve the size of the business's product range. This meant the business would be returning to its original range of Indian ready meals.

	2022	2023	2024
Tomatoes per tonne	£1590.00	£1630.00	£1742.00
Rice per tonne	£268.00	£275.00	£300.00
Fennel seeds per kilo	£12.50	£14.80	£17.25
Garlic powder per kilo	£5.00	£6.20	£7.00

▲ **Table 1** The rising cost of four of Shiaz's main ingredients

---

21.4 Give *one* product that Shiaz produces in its factory. **(1)**

21.5 Using the information in Table 1, calculate the average price of tomatoes per tonne from 2022 to 2024. You are advised to show your workings. **(2)**

21.6 Using the information in Table 1, calculate, to two decimal places, the percentage increase in the cost of garlic powder from 2022 to 2024. You are advised to show your workings. **(2)**

> **EXAM TIP**
>
> To calculate percentage change:
> 1. calculate the difference between the two values: original value − the new value
> 2. divide the difference by the original value
> 3. multiply the result by 100 to express it as a percentage.

21.7 As a result of the problems it faced in 2024, Shiaz changed its aims and objectives from increasing its product range to decreasing its product range.

Analyse the impact on Shiaz of changing its aims and objectives to decreasing its product range. **(6)**

Knowledge

22 Business and globalisation

The impact of globalisation on businesses

Globalisation has created opportunities and threats for UK businesses. It has led to greater interconnectedness between countries, resulting in more international trade. For UK businesses, this means more opportunities to sell abroad, but also more competition at home.

> **REMEMBER**
> Be careful not to confuse imports and exports. Imports are coming into a country. Exports are exiting a country.

Imports and exports

Imports are products flowing into a country. Globalisation has increased imports into the UK.
- It is easier for UK businesses to buy raw materials or finished goods from overseas and import them into the UK, where they can sell them.
- It is easier for foreign businesses to sell products in the UK, creating competition for UK businesses.

Exports are products flowing out of a country. Globalisation has increased exports from the UK.
- It is easier for UK businesses to sell products abroad, increasing access to new markets.

Changing business locations

Globalisation has made it easier for UK businesses to relocate to another country to gain a competitive advantage. Reasons for relocating include:

- to benefit from lower costs, such as cheaper labour costs or cheaper rent
- to be closer to the target market
- to gain local expertise.

Multinationals

Globalisation has seen a rise in the number of **multinationals**. Multinationals are businesses that operate in more than one country. For example, they may have factories or retail outlets in both Europe and the USA.

The benefits of operating in more than one country include:

- lower costs because of the size of the business
- access to a bigger target market
- access to expertise in different countries
- greater overall brand recognition
- opportunities to spread risk, because it is possible that, as one market declines, another grows.

> **Key terms** Make sure you can write a definition for these key terms
>
> domestic business · globalisation · international trade · multinational · tariff · trade bloc

Barriers to international trade

International trade is the flow of products between countries.

While some countries see international trade as a good thing, others want to protect **domestic businesses** from increased competition. Barriers to international trade are obstacles that act to reduce the flow of trade between countries.

Tariffs

Tariffs are taxes charged on imports: when goods and services are imported into a country a tax is added, making them more expensive and, therefore, less competitive.

Tariffs may encourage customers to buy from domestic businesses, because the price of domestic goods and services are cheaper. However, this is not always the case, because imported goods and services may be more desirable and customers may be willing to pay more for them as a result.

Tariffs are also a source of income for governments.

Trade blocs

Trade blocs are groups of countries that work together to encourage trade between member countries, and to protect themselves from trade with countries outside the trade bloc. Examples include the European Union (EU) and the Association of Southeast Asian Nations (ASEAN).

Products can flow freely between members of the trade bloc, but tariffs are applied to goods and services from countries outside the bloc.

How businesses compete internationally

Businesses selling in international markets are often competing with domestic businesses. There are two main ways in which businesses compete internationally: using the internet and e-commerce, and changing the marketing mix.

LINK

You can find out more about the four elements of the marketing mix in Chapters 24–28.

Using the internet and e-commerce

The internet and e-commerce have broken down some of the traditional barriers to international trade, making it easier for businesses to enter new markets abroad.

It is now easier for businesses to advertise and sell products online, reaching customers across the globe 24/7. Businesses can also accept international payments, ship goods internationally, or make products instantly available to download or stream online.

Price
- Showing prices in a different currency, such as the Euro
- Charging a lower price to be competitive if, for example, there is already a lot of competition
- Charging a higher price to take tariffs or additional shipping costs into account

Product
- Adapting to legislation in different countries, such as permitted ingredients or labelling requirements
- Meeting international manufacturing standards
- Matching the needs of the market, such as adjusting the number of items in a pack because families tend to be bigger or smaller
- Adapting to cultural or religious needs, such as using Halal ingredients

Place
- Using e-commerce
- Selling through a business located in the target country, because it understands the market better

Examples of how the marketing mix can be changed to make products and services more attractive to international markets

Promotion
- Reflecting the ethnic mix in different countries
- Reflecting the languages spoken in different countries
- Responding to different cultures in different countries
- Responding to social trends in different countries

Retrieval

Answer the questions below. Cover the answers column with a piece of paper and write down as many answers as you can. Check and repeat.

Questions & Answers

#	Questions	Answers
1	What does globalisation mean for UK businesses?	More opportunities to sell abroad, but also more competition at home
2	What are imports?	Products flowing into a country
3	What are exports?	Products flowing out of a country
4	What are businesses that operate in more than one country called?	Multinationals
5	State one impact of globalisation on businesses.	One from: increased imports into the UK / increased exports from the UK / easier for UK businesses to relocate to another country to gain competitive advantage / rise in the number of multinationals
6	Give one reason why a business might want to set up a factory in another country.	One from: to benefit from lower costs, such as cheaper labour costs or cheaper rent / to be closer to the target market / to gain local expertise
7	Why might a country want to create barriers to international trade?	To protect domestic businesses from increased competition
8	What is a tariff?	A tax charged on imports
9	What is a trade bloc?	A group of countries that work together to encourage trade between member countries, and to protect themselves from trade with countries outside the trade bloc
10	State two ways that businesses compete internationally.	Using the internet and e-commerce; changing the marketing mix

Previous questions

Use the questions below to check your knowledge from previous chapters.

#	Questions	Answers
1	What is a public limited company?	A business that can sell shares on a stock market, and has limited liability
2	Give three external reasons why business aims and objectives change as businesses evolve.	Market conditions; technology; legislation
3	If a business changes its aims and objectives to increase the use of machinery, what might happen to the size of the workforce?	The size of the workforce may be reduced

22 Business and globalisation

Practice 22

Exam-style questions

22.1 Which *one* of the following is an example of an import? (1)

    A A UK business sells soft drinks to France

    B A UK business sells over the internet

    C A UK business buys raw materials from Italy

    D A UK business relocates to Vietnam

22.2 Which *two* of the following are barriers to international trade? (2)

    A Exports   **D** Tariffs

    B Changing business location   **E** Trade blocs

    C E-commerce

22.3 Explain *one* method a business can use to grow externally. (3)

22.4 Discuss the impact of globalisation on businesses. (6)

> **EXAM TIP**
> Remember, impacts can be positive and/or negative.

> IT4U is a UK-based business that repairs electronic devices, including mobile phones, laptops and games consoles. A customer registers their faulty product online and posts it to IT4U. IT4U then provides the customer with a price that the customer agrees to before the repair is carried out. Prices are more competitive than high street stores due to lower overhead costs. IT4U buys small electrical components, such as chips, circuit boards, and wires, from Asia.

22.5 State *one* product that IT4U imports. (1)

22.6 Outline *one* way that IT4U has benefitted from globalisation. (2)

> **EXAM TIP**
> You must include context in your answers to 'Outline' questions. This means you need to make two references to IT4U in your answer to this question.

22.7 Outline *one* drawback to IT4U of the UK government introducing tariffs on imports from Asia. (2)

22.8 Evaluate whether importing materials from abroad is the main factor contributing to IT4U's competitive advantage. (12)

Knowledge

23 Ethics, the environment and business

The impact of ethical and environmental considerations on businesses

Business activity is influenced by ethical and environmental considerations.

Ethical considerations

Ethical considerations involve businesses acting in a way that is generally seen as morally correct and in line with moral principles.

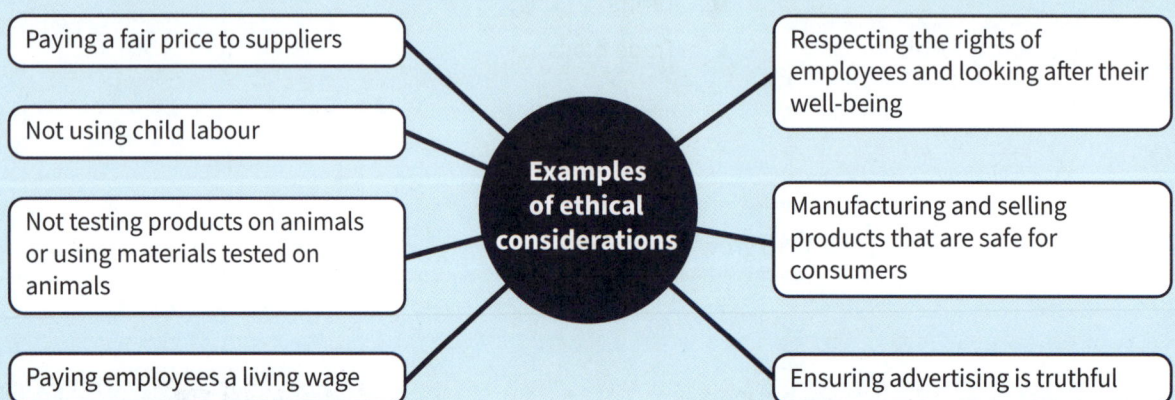

Examples of ethical considerations:
- Paying a fair price to suppliers
- Not using child labour
- Not testing products on animals or using materials tested on animals
- Paying employees a living wage
- Respecting the rights of employees and looking after their well-being
- Manufacturing and selling products that are safe for consumers
- Ensuring advertising is truthful

Environmental considerations

Environmental considerations involve businesses acting in a way that reduces the negative impact they have on the planet.

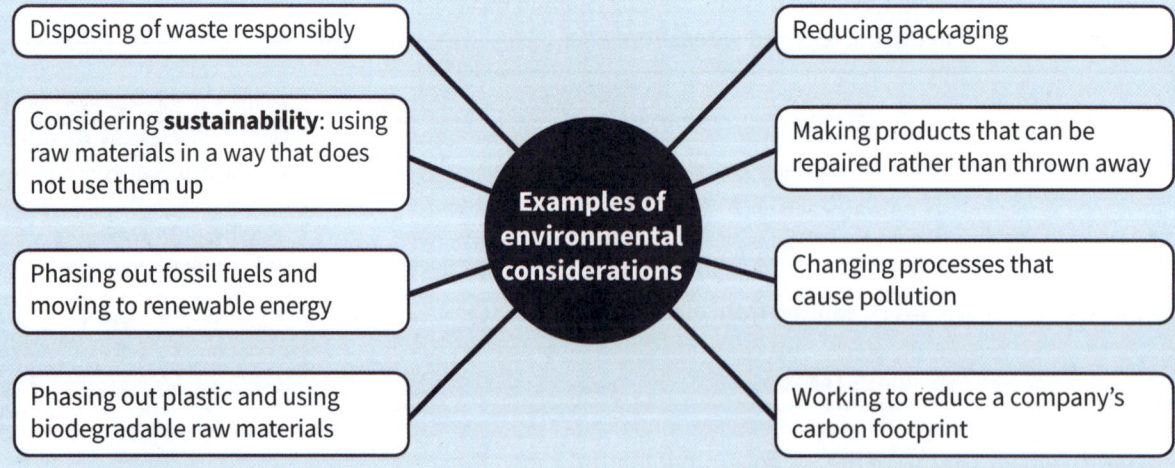

Examples of environmental considerations:
- Disposing of waste responsibly
- Considering **sustainability**: using raw materials in a way that does not use them up
- Phasing out fossil fuels and moving to renewable energy
- Phasing out plastic and using biodegradable raw materials
- Reducing packaging
- Making products that can be repaired rather than thrown away
- Changing processes that cause pollution
- Working to reduce a company's carbon footprint

Key terms — Make sure you can write a definition for these key terms:

environmental consideration   ethical consideration   sustainability   trade-off

Trade-offs

A **trade-off** occurs when a business has to give up one thing in return for another.

- A business may decide to trade off (give up) profit in return for meeting ethical and environmental aims and objectives.
- A business may decide to trade off (give up) on its ethical and environmental aims and objectives in return for profit.

Possible trade-offs between ethics and profit

Behaving ethically can increase costs.

For example, paying a fair price to suppliers can mean a business is paying more for goods or services than its competitors. If these higher costs are not passed on to the consumer in the form of higher prices, it will lead to lower profit.

As a result, the business needs to trade off between ethics and profit. It needs to decide if it wants to sacrifice profit in order to meet its ethical aims and objectives or vice versa.

Possible trade-offs between the environment, sustainability and profit

Behaving in an environmentally-friendly, sustainable way to protect nature and prevent the Earth's resources from being used up can increase costs.

For example, disposing of waste responsibly can mean a business spends more on waste disposal than a competitor that does not care so much about the environment and sustainability. If this higher cost is not passed on to the consumer in the form of higher prices, it will lead to lower profit.

As a result, the business needs to trade off between the environment and sustainability, and profit. It needs to decide if it wants to sacrifice profit in order to meet its environmental and sustainability aims and objectives or vice versa.

It is important to note that there is not always a trade-off between profit and ethical and environmentally-friendly considerations. Many consumers are happy to pay higher prices to purchase products that match their own ethical and environmental values.

Business activity that is ethical and minimises its impact on the environment can enhance the reputation of a business, leading to positive word of mouth publicity, positive reviews on social media, and brand loyalty.

> **REVISION TIP**
>
> Read exam questions carefully. Although there is clearly some overlap between ethical and environmental considerations, a question may want an answer that is clearly focussed on one or the other.

The potential impact of pressure group activity on the marketing mix

Pressure groups are organisations that try to influence the behaviour of consumers, businesses and governments. They normally have a specific ethical or environmental goal. For example, fairtrade pressure groups fight to ensure standards, as well as fair prices and conditions for farmers and workers.

Pressure group activities include:

- media campaigns to promote their goal, including social media campaigns
- protests to draw the issue to public attention
- boycotts, calling on consumers not to buy the products from a specific business in the hope of persuading it to change its practices.

The actions of pressure groups can impact the marketing mix. For example:

- Product: a business decides to swap to ethically- and sustainably-sourced materials.
- Price: a business decides to charge higher prices to cover the cost of paying a fair price to suppliers.
- Promotion: a business decides to emphasise the way it has changed its behaviour or highlight ethical and environmental practices in its promotional campaigns.
- Place: a business relocates, moving closer to its main market to reduce its carbon footprint.

Retrieval

Answer the questions below. Cover the answers column with a piece of paper and write down as many answers as you can. Check and repeat.

	Questions	Answers
1	What is meant by 'ethical considerations'?	Acting in a way that is seen as morally correct and in line with moral principles
2	What is meant by 'environmental considerations'?	Acting in a way that reduces the negative impact on the planet
3	How can a business act sustainably?	By using raw materials in a way that does not use them up
4	What is a trade-off?	When a business has to give up one thing in return for another
5	How do businesses trade off between ethical/ environmental considerations and profit?	Behaving ethically / in an environmentally-friendly way can increase costs. As a result, a business needs to decide if it wants to sacrifice profit in order to meet its ethical / environmental aims and objectives or vice versa
6	Why is there not always a trade-off between profit and ethical and environmental values?	Because many consumers are happy to pay higher prices to purchase products that match their own ethical and environmental values
7	What is a pressure group?	An organisation that tries to influence the behaviour of consumers, businesses, and governments
8	Give two examples of pressure group activities.	Two from: media campaigns, including social media campaigns / protests / boycotts
9	Give one example of how the actions of a pressure group can impact on the product element of the marketing mix.	A business decides to swap to ethically- and sustainably-sourced materials

Previous questions

Use the questions below to check your knowledge from previous chapters.

	Questions	Answers
1	What are business aims and objectives?	The goals and targets a business sets for itself
2	What are imports?	Products flowing into a country
3	Give one reason why a business might want to set up a factory in another country.	One from: to benefit from lower costs, such as cheaper labour costs or cheaper rent / to be closer to the target market / to gain local expertise

23 Ethics, the environment and business

Practice 23

Exam-style questions

23.1 Which *one* of the following is an ethical consideration influencing business activity? **(1)**

- A Reducing the amount of pollution created
- B Looking after the well-being of employees
- C Using biodegradable raw materials
- D Ignoring pressure group activity

23.2 Which *two* of the following are environmental considerations influencing business activity? **(2)**

- A Sourcing materials locally
- B Not testing on animals
- C Reducing profit
- D Using less packaging
- E Paying workers fairly

23.3 Explain *one* way that pressure group activities can impact on a business's marketing mix. **(3)**

23.4 Explain *one* way stakeholders are affected by business activity. **(3)**

23.5 Discuss how ethical considerations influence business activity. **(6)**

> Baby Panda is a manufacturer of designer clothes for babies. It is thinking of making all its goods – including socks, reusable nappies, dresses, shorts, and t-shirts – from bamboo. Bamboo grows quickly and is farmed without the use of pesticides so it can be more sustainable than cotton.
>
> Baby Panda's new range of bamboo baby clothes will target customers who care about the environment. Its prices will be high compared to other leading designer brands. For example, a competitor's cotton dress sells for £25.99 while an equivalent dress made from bamboo will sell for £40 at Baby Panda.

23.6 State *one* product that Baby Panda will manufacture out of bamboo. **(1)**

23.7 Calculate how much more expensive Baby Panda's bamboo dress will be than its competitor's cotton dress, expressed as a percentage to two decimal places. You are advised to show your working. **(2)**

23.8 Outline *one* possible trade-off Baby Panda could make between environmental considerations and profit. **(2)**

23.9 Evaluate whether Baby Panda will benefit from manufacturing products out of bamboo. You should use the information provided as well as your knowledge of business. **(12)**

> **EXAM TIP**
> Your answers to 'Evaluate' questions should be balanced. Remember to consider both sides of the argument before reaching a conclusion.

Exam-style questions

Sandcastle Ltd owns 23 holiday parks on the south coast of England. Each site offers customers pitches for tents and caravans, as well as a swimming pool, a play park, a restaurant and nightly live entertainment. The main target market is young families.

Rising costs have put pressure on Sandcastle Ltd's profits. Bea, the managing director, does not want to put prices up. She strongly believes that young families should be able to enjoy a holiday in the UK and doesn't want to make staying at Sandcastle Ltd's holiday parks too expensive.

Despite falling profits, Bea has an aim of growth. An opportunity has arisen for a merger with a smaller business, Waltzers Ltd. Waltzers Ltd operates ten holiday parks on the east coast of England. Its parks tend to be smaller and have fewer facilities: they do not have swimming pools and do not offer live entertainment. The merged businesses will operate under the new name Sandcastles and Waltzers Ltd.

Waltzers Ltd has an excellent reputation as an environmentally-friendly business. All fruit and vegetables used in its restaurants are grown on site. This helps keep costs down. It also encourages customers to recycle waste products and has banned single-use plastics in its shops and restaurants. Waltzers Ltd's profits have been steady in recent years.

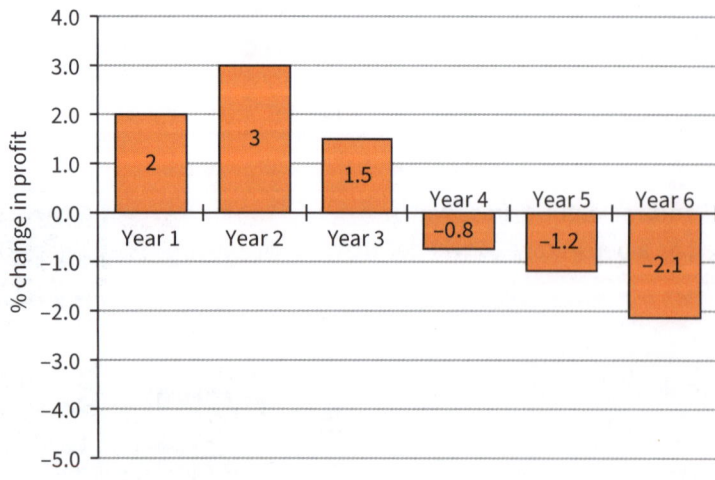

▲ **Figure 1** *The percentage change in profit for Sandcastle Ltd over the last six years*

23.10 Define the term 'merger'. (1)

23.11 Using the information in Figure 1, identify the year with the largest percentage change in Sandcastle Ltd's profit. (1)

23.12 Outline *one* benefit to Waltzer Ltd of its ban on single-use plastics in its shops and restaurants. (2)

> **EXAM TIP**
>
> When marking 'Justify' questions, the examiner is looking for balance. This means that you must present both sides of the argument. For example, if you choose Option 1, you should write one paragraph about the advantage of Option 1 and a second paragraph about the disadvantage of Option 1.

23.13 Ensuring the facilities offered across all 33 sites are the same is estimated to cost £2.2 million. Sandcastles and Waltzers Ltd has considered two options to raise the necessary finance:

Option 1: retained profit

Option 2: stock market flotation.

Justify which *one* of these two options Sandcastles and Waltzers Ltd should choose. (9)

> **EXAM TIP**
>
> When answering 'Evaluate' questions, look for evidence in the case study to support your argument. For example, after the merger Sandcastles and Waltzers Ltd will have 33 sites on the south coast and the east coast of England. How will this help increase profit? However, Sandcastles Ltd has seen profits fall for each of the last three years, so how will the company finance the merger?

23.14 Evaluate whether the merger is likely to lead to higher profits for Sandcastles and Waltzers Ltd. You should use the information provided as well as your knowledge of business. (12)

Knowledge

24 Product

Making marketing decisions

As a business grows, it needs to make decisions about the marketing mix. These decisions influence how the business attracts and maintains customers.

LINK

It is important to understand how each of the 4Ps of the marketing mix contribute to the success of a business. Revisit the concept of the marketing mix in Chapter 13.

What is product?

Product is one of the four Ps of the marketing mix.

Products are the goods and/or services that a business sells to its customers. For example, a supermarket sells a large range of products, including clothes, stationery, fruit and vegetables, and frozen foods. For example, a firm of lawyers sells legal advice to its clients.

The design mix

When designing products, a business considers the **design mix**. This helps the business attract customers with a desirable product, while still being able to make a profit. There are three elements to the design mix: function, aesthetics, and cost.

Function
What does the product do?
What features does it have?
How is it different to similar products on the market?
What will customers want to gain from owning the product?

Aesthetics
How does the product look?
How does the product feel?
How does the product smell?
Is the product attractive to customers?

Cost
Is the product viable: what is the cost of production?
Is there scope to make a profit?

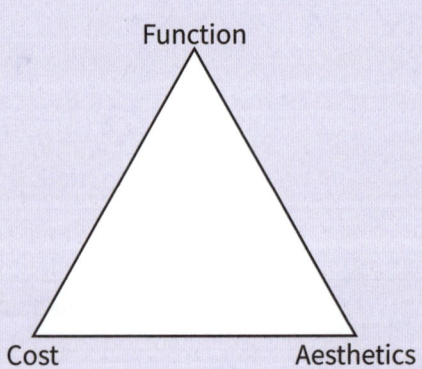

REVISION TIP

Consider the design mix in relation to a number of products you own, such as a phone, an item of clothing, an item of stationery. For each product, think about the importance of each aspect of the design mix. This will help you think about context when you come to answer Section B and Section C questions in your exams.

Key terms — Make sure you can write a definition for these key terms

design mix   extension strategy   product life cycle

The product life cycle

The **product life cycle** refers to the stages a product goes through over the course of its life, from its launch all the way through to its eventual decline.

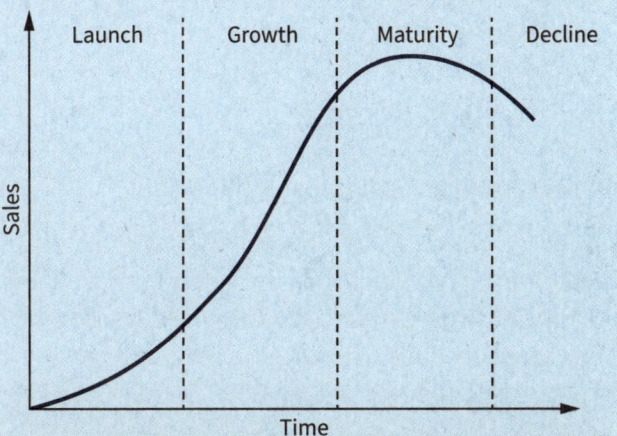

Launch
The product has been developed and is first made available for sale. There is likely to be heavy investment in promoting the product to create awareness. Cash flow is likely to be negative because promotional expenditure is high and sales are relatively low. However, if the launch has been eagerly awaited by customers (e.g. if it is the launch of a new computer game), initial sales may be high.

Growth
As customers become increasingly aware of the product, sales should start to increase. This will increase sales revenue. Promotional expenditure may start to fall as the business no longer needs to work so hard to raise awareness of the product.

Maturity
Sales reach their highest point and the product is now bringing profit into the business. Promotion will continue, to try and maintain the maturity stage for as long as possible.

Decline
Sales start to fall and the business needs to decide whether or not to continue selling the product. The product may now have a negative cash flow.

Extension strategies

Extension strategies are actions taken by a business to extend the maturity stage of the product life cycle. They help stop a product entering the decline stage of the product life cycle. Examples of extension strategies include:

- changing the product (e.g, introducing new flavours of ice cream)
- updating the packaging
- introducing new features or functions
- launching a new advertising campaign or a new pricing strategy
- changing the target market.

Why do businesses differentiate their products?

Businesses operate in a competitive environment. Therefore, they want to have a competitive advantage: they want to be better than other businesses operating in the same market. One way to achieve this is through product differentiation.

Product differentiation makes a business's products stand out from its competitors' products, and many businesses identify a unique selling point (USP) to make their products more desirable.

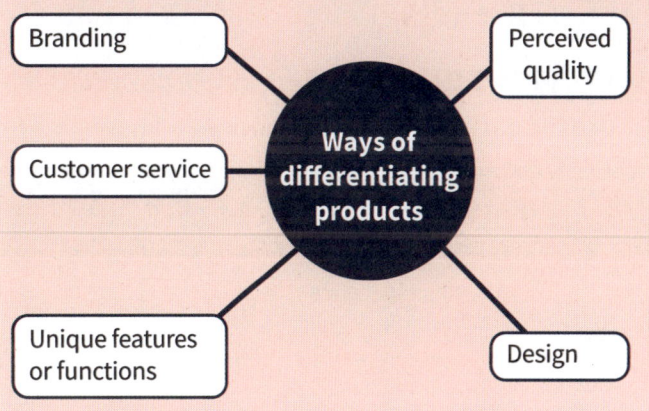

24 Knowledge

Retrieval

Answer the questions below. Cover the answers column with a piece of paper and write down as many answers as you can. Check and repeat.

Questions	Answers
1. What are products?	The goods and / or services that a business sells to its customers
2. What are the three elements of the design mix?	Function; aesthetics; cost
3. Give two questions a business asks itself when it is considering the cost of a product.	Is the product viable: what is the cost of production? Is there scope to make a profit?
4. What is the product life cycle?	The stages a product goes through over the course of its life, from its launch all the way through to its eventual decline
5. At what stage of the product life cycle are sales at their lowest?	Launch
6. At what stage of the product life cycle are sales at their highest?	Maturity
7. What is an extension strategy?	An action taken by a business to extend the maturity stage of the product life cycle
8. Give three examples of an extension strategy.	Three from: changing the product / updating the packaging / introducing new features or functions / launching a new advertising campaign or a new pricing strategy / changing the target market
9. What is product differentiation?	A business making its products stand out from competitors' products
10. What is a USP?	A unique selling point
11. Give two ways a business can differentiate its products.	Two from: branding / customer service / unique features or functions / perceived quality / design

Previous questions

Use the questions below to check your knowledge from previous chapters.

Questions	Answers
1. What is the marketing mix?	The key elements of a marketing plan: price, product, promotion and place work together to create a single message to attract customers
2. The marketing mix is adapted to a product depending on how much money the business has to spend on marketing and a number of other factors. Name three of these factors.	Competitive environment; changing consumer needs; technology
3. What is meant by 'environmental considerations'?	Acting in a way that reduces the negative impact on the planet

Practice 24

Exam-style questions

24.1 Which *one* of the following is part of the design mix? **(1)**
- **A** Price
- **B** Marketing
- **C** Function
- **D** Product

24.2 Which *two* of the following are stages found in the product life cycle? **(2)**
- **A** Aesthetics
- **B** Decline
- **C** Differentiation
- **D** Design mix
- **E** Launch

24.3 Explain *one* benefit to a business of using the design mix. **(3)**

24.4 Explain *one* benefit to a business of exporting its products overseas. **(3)**

24.5 Discuss the importance to a business of understanding the product life cycle. **(6)**

> Agri-Jam plc is a leading brand of jams stocked in three of the major supermarkets in the UK. Unlike other jams, it uses natural sweeteners rather than added sugars. This means that Agri-Jam plc's products are healthier than those of its competitors. However, leading competitors are starting to introduce healthier options. This has reduced Agri-Jam plc's market share. Agri-Jam plc's annual sales have fallen by 30% during the last three years.
>
> Agri-Jam plc grows a lot of its ingredients in greenhouses in the UK. However, more unusual fruits, such as mango and papaya, are imported. The company pays farmers in Asia a fair price for the imported fruits as part of its ethical policies.

EXAM TIP

When reading a case study, annotate important information by asking yourself: Why is this important? For example, you might annotate 'leading brand' with 'well recognised' or 'well known'.

24.6 Outline *one* advantage to Agri-Jam plc of being ethical. **(2)**

24.7 Outline *one* unique selling point of Agri-Jam plc's jam. **(2)**

24.8 Analyse the importance to Agri-Jam plc of product differentiation. **(6)**

24.9 In order to increase sales, Agri-Jam plc's marketing manager is considering the following options:

Option 1: changing the packaging, from jars to single-serve sachets

Option 2: launching a new range of fruit-based sweets for children.

Justify which *one* of these two options Agri-Jam Plc should choose. **(9)**

Knowledge

25 Price

What is price?

Price is one of the four Ps of the marketing mix.

The price is the amount a business charges its customers for a product.

Pricing strategies

A business needs to decide what price to charge its customers. The price should be high enough to cover costs and allow the business to make a profit and survive. It must also be set at a level that will attract customers; this is especially important in a competitive market.

A pricing strategy is the plan a business puts together to determine the prices that should be set for its products. A business will choose either a high-price strategy or a low-price strategy.

Influences on pricing strategies

There are four influences on pricing strategies: technology, competition, market segments, and product lifestyle.

Technology

Technology is likely to affect the function element of the design mix positively: the product will have more features to appeal to the customer. This will lead to product differentiation.

As a result, customers are more likely to pay a higher price to be one of the first to own the product. The high price will help the business recover the high research and development costs associated with designing a technologically-advanced product.

Competition

A business may set the same price, or a similar price, to that of its competitors. This is particularly true if there is little product differentiation.

If a business sets the price below that of its competitors others may follow, leading to a price war. This benefits the customer but not the businesses involved: the customer pays less while the businesses receive lower sales revenue.

Market segmentation

Different target markets have different amounts of disposable income and attitudes to price. For example, if the target market is older customers with a higher level of income, a business may set a high price. If, however, the target market is young teenagers, a business is more likely to set a lower price.

Product life cycle

When a product is first launched, a high price may be set to attract early adopters: customers who are willing to pay a high price to be one of the first to own the product. As the product moves into the growth and maturity stages of the product life cycle, the price may be lowered to encourage more customers to purchase it as the customers who were willing to pay a high price already have it.

If a product is aimed at a wide target market, a low price may be set when it is launched to encourage the maximum number of customers to try it. As the product moves into the growth and then the maturity stages of the product life cycle, the price may be increased because customers who already like it may be willing to pay more to continue to buy it.

> **REVISION TIP**
>
> In Chapter 5, you looked at five ways to identify market segments. Consider how location, demographics, lifestyle, income, and age influence whether a business sets a high price or a low price.

Retrieval 25

Answer the questions below. Cover the answers column with a piece of paper and write down as many answers as you can. Check and repeat.

Questions | Answers

1. What is meant by the term 'price'? — It is the amount a business charges its customers for a product

2. What is a pricing strategy? — The plan a business puts together to determine the prices that should be set for its products

3. There are two pricing strategies. What are they? — A high-price strategy and a low-price strategy

4. How does technology influence the choice of pricing strategy? — Customers are more likely to pay a higher price to be one of the first to own a technologically-advanced product

5. In addition to technology, give three other influences on pricing strategies. — Competition; market segments; product life cycle

Previous questions

Use the questions below to check your knowledge from previous chapters.

Questions | Answers

1. What are the three elements of market segmentation? — Identify specific customer requirements; create distinct market segments; market specific products to each market segment

2. What is the product life cycle? — The stages a product goes through over the course of its life, from its launch all the way through to its eventual decline

Practice

Exam-style questions

25.1 Explain *one* advantage to a business of setting a low price. (3)

25.2 Explain *one* trade-off between profit and ethics. (3)

25.3 Discuss how the number of competitors in a market affects the choice of pricing strategy. (6)

 # Knowledge

26 Promotion

What is promotion?

Promotion is one of the four Ps of the marketing mix.

Promotion is the activities a business carries out to raise awareness of its products and to encourage customers to make a purchase. Promotion can be informative and/or persuasive.

Promotional strategies

Businesses have a range of promotional strategies to choose from and they select the ones that are most appropriate for the market segment they are targeting.

Advertising	Using media to communicate with potential customers, including billboards, newspapers, television, radio, websites, and social media.	**Special offers**	Encouraging customers to make a purchase there and then, or to buy more than they normally would. For example, offering a discount if customers buy today, or offering a multiple-purchase discount such as three for the price of two.
Sponsorship	Providing finance to an organisation, group or event in return for displaying the business's name or one of its brands in a prominent position. For example, a business may sponsor a charity event, a sports club or a community group.	**Branding**	Using a unique feature to distinguish products from competitors' products. This could include a logo, a shape, a colour, a sound, or a function. Customers are attracted to the brand and may become loyal to it.
Product trials	Encouraging customers to try a product for free for a short period of time before they have to commit to buying it. For example, a 30-day free trial of a subscription to a streaming service.		

> **REVISION TIP**
>
> When revising promotional strategies, consider the nature of the product and the target market. Ask yourself 'To whom would this method of promotion be appropriate?'

The use of technology in promotion

Businesses can use technology in their promotion. It provides a cost-effective way to reach a large number of existing and potential customers.

Targeted advertising online	**Viral advertising via social media**	**E-newsletters**
Websites track searches to identify preferences and interests. Businesses can use this information, stored in cookies, to send potential customers tailored adverts. This helps increase the effectiveness of online adverts.	Businesses use social media platforms to share promotional offers and product information. People can respond and share posts with their own networks. This means the message spreads quickly, reaching a large number of potential customers.	Businesses can build a database by asking people to subscribe to an e-newsletter. Regular updates and offers can then be sent quickly to all subscribers by email.

Retrieval 26

Answer the questions below. Cover the answers column with a piece of paper and write down as many answers as you can. Check and repeat.

Questions | Answers

1 What is meant by the term 'promotion'? | Promotion is the activities a business carries out to raise awareness of its products and to encourage customers to make a purchase

2 State three promotion strategies. | Three from: advertising / sponsorship / product trials / special offers / branding

3 What is advertising? | Using media to communicate with potential customers, including billboards, newspapers, television, radio, websites, and social media

4 What is sponsorship? | Providing finance for an organisation, group or event in return for displaying the business's name or one of its brands in a prominent position

5 Give three ways technology is used in promotion. | Targeted advertising online; viral advertising via social media; e-newsletters

Previous questions

Use the questions below to check your knowledge from previous chapters.

Questions | Answers

1 What are products? | The goods and/or services that a business sells to its customers

2 What is product differentiation? | A business making its products stand out from competitors' products

Practice

Exam-style questions

26.1 Explain *one* influence on a business's choice of pricing strategy. (3)

26.2 Discuss the impact on a business of using special offers as a promotional method. (6)

Knowledge

27 Place

What is place?

Place is one of the 4Ps of the marketing mix.

Place is how products are sold and distributed to customers.

How businesses distribute their products

Some businesses have a short distribution channel. For example:

producer/provider → customer

Other businesses will have a longer distribution channel. For example:

producer/provider → **wholesaler** → retailer/e-tailer → customer

> **REVISION TIP**
>
> Increasingly, businesses are using a combination of retail and e-tail to distribute their products. This is called 'clicks and bricks'. Consider why a growing business might benefit from using both methods of distribution.

Methods of distribution

Businesses can choose to sell their products through retailers, e-tailers (e-commerce), or a mixture of both.

Retailers	E-tailers (e-commerce)
Retailers have a physical location, such as a high street store, a village shop or a market stall.	E-tailers sell over the internet; they do not have a physical location.
Advantages and disadvantages	**Advantages and disadvantages**
✓ Face-to-face interaction with customers allows for high levels of customer service. ✓ Customers may enjoy the shopping experience, leading to repeat business. ✓ Personal services, such as hairdressing and other health and beauty treatments, require a physical location. ✗ It can be expensive to operate because of the high overhead costs. ✗ Opening hours are usually limited, which can be inconvenient for customers. ✗ The geographical area the business can trade in may be limited by the number of shops it can open.	✓ Lower overhead costs, leading to lower prices or higher profits ✓ Greater convenience for customers, who can access the website 24/7, encouraging sales ✓ Can reach a wide geographical area, potentially achieving global sales ✗ Higher number of returns increases operational costs, especially in the clothing industry where customers order multiple sizes intending to return some of them ✗ Difficult to form strong relationships with customers, making it harder to gain their loyalty ✗ Some customers may lack confidence with, for example, online payment systems, leading to a loss in sales

Key terms — Make sure you can write a definition for these key terms: e-tailer, wholesaler

# Retrieval 27

Answer the questions below. Cover the answers column with a piece of paper and write down as many answers as you can. Check and repeat.

Questions | Answers

1 What is meant by the term 'place'? | Place is how products are sold and distributed to customers

2 What is a retailer? | A business that sells goods and services from a physical location

3 What is an e-tailer? | A business that sells goods or services over the internet; does not have a physical location

4 Give one advantage of using e-tailers as a method of distribution. | One from: lower overhead costs, leading to lower prices or higher profits / greater convenience for customers, who can access the website 24/7, encouraging sales / can reach a wide geographical area, potentially achieving global sales

Previous questions
Use the questions below to check your knowledge from previous chapters.

Questions | Answers

1 There are two pricing strategies. What are they? | A high-price strategy and a low-price strategy

2 What is advertising? | Using media to communicate with potential customers, including billboards, newspapers, television, radio, websites, and social media

# Practice

Exam-style questions

27.1 Explain *one* disadvantage to a business of using e-commerce to distribute products. **(3)**

27.2 Explain *one* benefit to a business of using technology in promotion. **(3)**

27.3 Discuss why a business may choose to distribute products using both retail and e-tail. **(6)**

Knowledge

28 Using the marketing mix to make business decisions

How each element of the marketing mix influences other elements

To be effective, the elements of the marketing mix must complement each other. For example, charging a high price for a poor-quality product that is advertised on a bench at a bus stop is unlikely to attract customers successfully.

As a result, each element of the marketing mix influences the others. If one element of the marketing mix is changed, this has an effect on the other elements. For example, if the price of a product is lowered, this may influence the retailers that are willing to stock it.

A designer fashion business has a highly-recognised brand. Its clothes are made using top-quality fabrics.

LINK

Before revising how the marketing mix is used to make decisions, have another look at Chapters 24–27 to remind yourself of the four elements of the marketing mix: product, price, promotion, and place.

Product
The product is a high-quality men's designer jacket. It is costly to produce because of the quality of the materials used and the skilled designer and tailors involved in making it. The product influences the other elements of the marketing mix.

Price
The price is influenced by the product. It is high to reflect the top-quality fabrics used to make the product, and the brand.

Promotion
The promotion is influenced by the product and the price. The product is high quality and this led the business to set a high price. The promotion must be appropriate to the product and attractive to high-income earners who can afford to buy it. For example, adverts could be placed in high-profile fashion magazines.

Place
Place is influenced by the price. A high-priced product should be displayed with care in places that attract customers with high levels of disposable income. These customers want to feel valued when making a purchase, so the product could be sold by a small number of boutique fashion retailers and e-tailers, as well as top department stores. High-profile fashion magazines do not promote clothing sold in supermarkets.

Using an integrated marketing mix to gain a competitive advantage

A business has a competitive advantage when customers think its products are better value or better quality than its competitors' products. Therefore, a business designs its marketing mix to give it a competitive advantage, with each element working to support the other three. This is known as an integrated marketing mix.

LINK

Revise the design mix in Chapter 24. How can the design mix be used when developing new products to gain a competitive advantage?

If a business manages to make its products more attractive to customers, this can lead to brand loyalty, increased sales, and a bigger market share.

Product

More features; more functionality; better quality; more aesthetically pleasing; more ethical; more eco-friendly.

> For example: a 415 g tin of Heinz Beanz, with a 'rich, original taste' that guarantees a quick and tasty meal when you're in a hurry

Place

Offers a comfortable, fun or desirable customer experience; more convenient.

> For example: sold in physical stores that are convenient for customers looking for a quick and tasty meal, like Tesco Metros

Price

Priced below competitors' prices if the product is perceived to be of equal quality; priced above competitors' prices to give the perception of better quality.

> For example: priced higher than supermarket own-brand baked beans because of the perceived quality of the 'rich, original taste'

Promotion

Increases brand recognition and brand loyalty, making the product more desirable.

> For example: two-for-one promotions encourage purchases but maintain the high price for perceived quality

Retrieval

Answer the questions below. Cover the answers column with a piece of paper and write down as many answers as you can. Check and repeat.

Questions / Answers

#	Question	Answer
1	How do the elements of the marketing mix relate to each other?	They must complement each other
2	When does a business have a competitive advantage?	When customers think its products are better value or better quality than its competitors' products
3	What is an integrated marketing mix?	A marketing mix where each element works to support the other three

Previous questions

Use the questions below to check your knowledge from previous chapters.

#	Question	Answer
1	What are the three elements of the design mix?	Function; aesthetics; cost
2	Give two questions a business asks itself when it is considering the cost of a product.	Is the product viable: what is the cost of production? Is there scope to make a profit?
3	Give two ways a business can differentiate its products.	Two from: branding / customer service / unique features or functions / perceived quality / design
4	What is a pricing strategy?	The plan a business puts together to determine the prices that should be set for its products
5	How does technology influence the choice of pricing strategy?	Customers are more likely to pay a higher price to be one of the first to own a technologically-advanced product
6	In addition to technology, give three other influences on pricing strategies.	Competition; market segments; product life cycle
7	State three promotion strategies.	Three from: advertising / sponsorship / product trials / special offers / branding
8	Give three ways technology is used in promotion.	Targeted advertising online; viral advertising via social media; e-newsletters
9	What is a retailer?	A business that sells goods and services from a physical location
10	What is an e-tailer?	A business that sells goods or services over the internet; does not have a physical location
11	Give one advantage of using e-tailers as a method of distribution.	One from: lower overhead costs, leading to lower prices or higher profits / greater convenience for customers, who can access the website 24/7, encouraging sales / can reach a wide geographical area, potentially achieving global sales

28 Using the marketing mix to make business decisions

Practice 28

Exam-style questions

28.1 Which *one* of the following is an element of the design mix? **(1)**

- A Product
- B Price
- C Aesthetics
- D E-commerce

28.2 Which *two* of the following are elements of the marketing mix? **(2)**

- A Function
- B Extension strategies
- C Promotion
- D Place
- E Cost

28.3 Explain *one* way a business can use the marketing mix to build a competitive advantage. **(3)**

28.4 Explain *one* way a business can use the design mix to build a competitive advantage. **(3)**

28.5 Discuss the impact on a business of an integrated marketing mix. **(6)**

Country Gent plc is a well-known men's fashion e-tailer. Its target market is high-income earners who live in the countryside, and its typical customer values Country Gent plc's traditional designs made from 100% English wool. The product range includes blazers, coats and waistcoats. A blazer retails at £650. Country Gent plc advertises in a popular magazine, *Horse & Hounds*, as well as sponsoring races at major horse-racing events, including events at York Racecourse and Royal Ascot. Country Gent plc's integrated marketing mix has given it a competitive advantage.

In recent years, the market has become more competitive, with other leading brands bringing out similar products. Jasper, the marketing director, has decided that it is time to lower the price of blazers to £599.

28.6 Define the term 'e-tailer'. **(1)**

28.7 Outline *one* way in which product has influenced the price of the £650 blazer in Country Gent plc's marketing mix. **(2)**

28.8 Analyse how each element of the marketing mix has contributed to Country Gent plc's competitive advantage. **(6)**

28.9 Evaluate the impact of changing the price of its blazers on Country Gent plc's ability to maintain its competitive advantage. You should use the information provided as well as your knowledge of business. **(12)**

> **EXAM TIP**
>
> 'Analyse' questions require you to provide context; to use information from the case study. Look at the case study and identify one piece of contextual information for each element of the marketing mix. These have been given to you deliberately. Do you think they fit well together? Include these pieces of contextual information in your answer as you develop your argument.

Practice

Exam-style questions

Deluxe Designs plc is a UK business that specialises in luxury handmade chocolates. It sells boxes of chocolates online and in high-end stores in London. It also has small stores in major UK airports. A major area of growth for the business in recent years has been to target the corporate gift-giving market. In the UK alone, businesses spend over £700 billion per year on sending gifts to valued customers and suppliers.

Deluxe Designs plc sells in over 100 countries worldwide. Since it was established in 2020, Deluxe Designs plc has sold to 500,000 online customers, with sales peaking each year around the Christmas holiday season.

Deluxe Designs plc uses social media to promote its products. It also asks online customers to sign up for monthly e-newsletters when they place an order.

Deluxe Designs plc is exploring the possibility of opening cafes alongside its small stores in major UK airports. It is currently trialling the concept in one airport.

Item	Price
Pot of English breakfast tea	£5.00
Slice of chocolate tart	£6.50
Salmon and cucumber sandwich	£11.00
Trio of chocolates	£6.60
Sparkling water	£4.50

▲ **Table 1** The price of items ordered by one customer in Deluxe Designs plc's airport cafe

28.10 Define the term *e-newsletter*. **(1)**

28.11 State *one* possible influence on the pricing strategy used by Deluxe Designs plc. **(1)**

28.12 Outline *one* benefit to Deluxe Designs plc of using e-commerce to sell its products. **(2)**

28.13 Using the information in Table 1, calculate the average price of the items ordered by the customer. You are advised to show your workings. **(2)**

> **EXAM TIP**
> To calculate an average, add up all the relevant values and divide the result by the number of values.

28.14 Analyse the impact to Deluxe Designs plc of using stores and e-commerce as methods of distribution. **(6)**

> **EXAM TIP**
> Look carefully at the case study to identify context you can use in your answer. Look at how many clues there are in just these two sentences:
>
> It sells boxes of chocolates online (reaching a wider audience, selling abroad, increasing revenue) and in high-end stores in London (reinforcing the brand's luxury image and ability to sell at high prices). It also has small stores in major UK airports (reaching tourists buying gifts to take home, reaching customers with high levels of disposable income).

28.15 In order to increase sales, Deluxe Designs plc is considering two options:

Option 1: introduce regular special offers

Option 2: open small retail stores in UK cities.

Justify which *one* of these two options Deluxe Designs plc should choose. **(9)**

28.16 Evaluate the impact on Deluxe Designs plc of having an integrated marketing mix. You should use the information provided as well as your knowledge of business. **(12)**

Knowledge

29 Business operations

The purpose of business operations

Business operations refer to the day-to-day activities of a business to meet its overall purpose. There are two main purposes of business:

To produce goods	To provide services
Goods are physical products; they can be touched. Examples include: • clothes • food • toys • electrical equipment.	Services are non-physical products; they cannot be touched. Examples include: • hair and beauty • hospitality • car repairs and servicing • professional services, such as solicitors and estate agents.

This does not mean a business must do one or the other; many businesses produce goods and provide services.

Production processes

Production processes are the methods a business uses to produce its products. The choice of process will be influenced by both the target market and the nature of the product.

There are three different methods of production: **job production**, **batch production** and **flow production**.

Job production	Batch production	Flow production
Each product is made individually. The products are one-off items tailored to meet specific customer requirements This method is used for specialist goods or personal services, such as wedding dresses, bespoke paint for cars, and dentistry.	Products are made in groups or batches. The products move through the production process one batch at a time. This method is often used when a business has a range of products but wants each batch to be identical; examples include bakery goods and ceramics.	Products travel along a continuous production line and are produced on a large scale. This method of production is used for the mass production of identical items, and machinery is often used a lot; examples include soft drinks and cars.

Key terms Make sure you can write a definition for these key terms

batch production   flow production
job production   production process

The impact of different types of production process

Operational aims and objectives include:
- keeping productivity up (productivity is the output per unit of input; for example, labour productivity is how much an employee can produce)
- keeping costs down
- enabling a business to compete on price.

The production process selected has an impact on these aims and objectives.

> **REVISION TIP**
>
> Consider how the production process chosen by a business gives them a competitive advantage. This will help you explain why it was chosen.

Job production	Batch production	Flow production
Productivity is likely to be low, because each item is made individually to meet customer needs.	Productivity is higher than with job production, because products are made in groups or batches. There may, however, be some downtime as machinery is switched over from one batch of products to another.	Productivity is high, often because a large amount of machinery is used and there is a constant flow of production.
Because productivity is low, unit cost is likely to be high. However, set up costs may be low.	Costs can be kept down, because labour and machinery are shared between different products within a business's product range.	Despite an initially high set-up cost, unit cost is low.
Businesses will compete with high-quality, highly-differentiated products, rather than on price.	Businesses can compete by offering a variety of products with consistent quality within batches. There is an opportunity to compete on price, but this may not be the business's main competitive advantage.	Businesses will compete on price, operating in a mass market.

The impacts of technology on production

Technology is used in the production process. This can include automated production lines, stock control systems where stock is automatically reordered, and quality checks carried out by machines.

The use of technology has an impact on four factors:

- **Balancing cost**: businesses need to balance the set-up cost of introducing technology, which can be high, with the lower unit cost that results from increased productivity.
- **Productivity**: this is increased with technology. Although limited downtime may be needed while maintenance is carried out or when production lines are changed over, technology doesn't get sick or need a break like employees do.
- **Quality**: this is more consistent with technology because machines, unless programmed incorrectly, do not make mistakes. However, they can go wrong! Machinery can also be used to test quality; for example, to weigh products or test that a product works as it should.
- **Flexibility**: this can be increased with technology because machines can be switched from one product range to another (something that happens frequently in batch production, and in flow production too). Switching machines between production processes can also be quicker than training employees.

29 Knowledge

Retrieval

Answer the questions below. Cover the answers column with a piece of paper and write down as many answers as you can. Check and repeat.

#	Questions	Answers
1	What is meant by the term 'business operations'?	The day-to-day activities of a business to meet its overall purpose
2	State the two main purposes of business.	To produce goods; to provide services
3	What is the difference between goods and services?	Goods are physical products (they can be touched); services are non-physical products (they cannot be touched)
4	State three different methods of production.	Job production; batch production; flow production
5	Which production process is used for the production of one-off items?	Job production
6	Which production process is used when products are made in groups?	Batch production
7	Which production process is used to mass produce identical products?	Flow production
8	What is meant by the term 'productivity'?	The output per unit of input
9	The production process selected has an impact on which three operational aims and objectives?	Keeping productivity up; keeping costs down; enabling a business to compete on price
10	Which production process has the highest productivity?	Flow production
11	Which production process is likely to have the highest unit cost?	Job production
12	How will businesses using job production compete?	With high-quality, highly-differentiated products
13	Give four impacts of technology on production.	Balancing cost; productivity; quality; flexibility

Previous questions

Use the questions below to check your knowledge from previous chapters.

#	Questions	Answers
1	What does globalisation mean for UK businesses?	More opportunities to sell abroad, but also more competition at home
2	What is meant by 'ethical considerations'?	Acting in a way that is seen as morally correct and in line with moral principles
3	How can a business act sustainably?	By using raw materials in a way that does not use them up

Practice 29

Exam-style questions

29.1 Which *one* of the following is a purpose of business operations? **(1)**
- A To make a profit
- B To produce goods
- C To recruit workers
- D To carry out market research

29.2 Which *two* of the following are impacts of technology on production? **(2)**
- A More consistent quality
- B Better communication with customers
- C Being able to reach a wider target market
- D Greater productivity
- E Online payment systems

29.3 Explain *one* impact on a business of using job production. **(3)**

29.4 Discuss the impact on a business of differentiating its products. **(6)**

Middle Eastern Breads manufactures speciality breads traditionally eaten in the Middle East, such as pitta bread and za'atar bread. When the owners, Ash and Soria, moved to the UK in 2000, they found supermarket breads lacked flavour and quickly set up the business.

They make 12 different types of breads using batch production. Five of the breads are either gluten- or nut-free. To avoid the risk of gluten or nuts getting into these breads, they shut down the machines and clean them thoroughly before they are produced.

Their gluten-free pitta bread is their biggest selling item, accounting for 35% of their total sales. Soria thinks that, as more people become aware of the health benefits of a gluten-free diet, sales will continue to rise. She wants to introduce flow production. However, Ash is concerned that there is a lot of competition from businesses that make cheaper products that are sold to discount supermarkets such as Aldi and Lidl. He worries that changing the production process will be costly, and wants to explore ways to finance the proposal other than a bank loan.

29.5 Outline *one* reason why Middle Eastern Breads sells gluten- and nut-free breads. **(2)**

29.6 Outline *one* disadvantage to Middle Eastern Breads of using a bank loan to finance changing the production process. **(2)**

29.7 Analyse the benefit to Ash and Soria of using batch production. **(6)**

29.8 Evaluate whether the introduction of flow production would be the best option for Middle Eastern Breads to increase its profits. You should use the information provided as well as your knowledge of business. **(12)**

> **EXAM TIP**
> 'Evaluate' questions require you to write an extended answer. This means you must fully develop your arguments in the context of the case study, before writing a conclusion.

Knowledge

30 Working with suppliers

Managing stock

Stock held by a business can be raw materials or finished goods. Raw materials are bought from a supplier (a business that provides goods or services to another business).

It is important for a business to manage stock effectively to ensure it can meet the needs of its customers, while at the same time not holding too much stock, which can be costly.

Bar gate stock graphs

Businesses may use **bar gate stock graphs** to monitor the inflow and outflow of stock. Bar gate stock graphs provide a visual record of the:

- lead time: the time it takes from placing an order to taking delivery

   lead time = delivery date − date of order

   for example:
   - delivery date = day 20
   - date of order = day 10
   - therefore, lead time = day 20 − day 10 = 10 days

- reorder level: the level of stock that triggers an order for new stock to be placed
- minimum level: the lowest amount of stock that should be held. This may include buffer stock in case there are problems with stock deliveries
- reorder quantity: how much stock is ordered once the reorder level is reached.

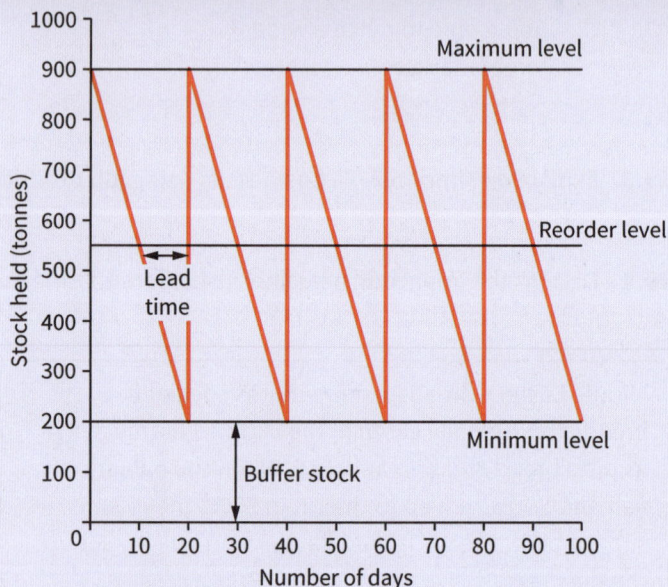
▲ A bar gate stock graph

> **REVISION TIP**
>
> You could be asked to read specific information off a bar stock graph in your exams, so practise interpreting them. For example, work out the lead time or identify the reorder level.

Just in time (JIT) stock control

Not all businesses hold buffer stock. Some businesses use a **just in time (JIT)** stock control system. This means that stock is delivered just as it is needed.

This method of stock control aims to minimise waste and reduce costs. However, there is a downside: if stock is not delivered on time, the business will fail to meet customer needs. This means JIT relies on excellent relationships with suppliers.

Just in time (JIT)
Advantages and disadvantages

Advantages	Disadvantages
✓ Lower storage costs, such as rent for warehousing, staff and insurance	✗ Need to handle more frequent deliveries
✓ Less risk of damage to stock	✗ Costs may be higher than buying in bulk
✓ No obsolete stock	✗ Risk of running out of stock if deliveries are disrupted
✓ Less cash tied up in holding stock	

The role of procurement

Procurement is the process of identifying suitable suppliers and buying the necessary goods or services from them. It is important to identify suppliers that can provide products that meet the needs of the business.

Relationships with suppliers

A business chooses its suppliers based upon a number of criteria. These include:

Quality	The products supplied are of the appropriate standard to consistently meet the expectations of the business.
Delivery (speed, reliability, cost)	The correct products are delivered to the business on time and at a reasonable cost. The farther away the supplier is from the business, the harder this is to achieve (if, for example, products have to be imported).
Availability	The supplier has the right products, in the correct quantities and at the appropriate quality, ready to deliver to the business.
Cost	The price paid by the business for delivery is a cost to the business. If the cost is high, this may have to be passed onto the customer in the form of higher prices, which could mean a loss of competitiveness.
Trust	The business needs to feel confident that the right products will be delivered on time. The business may want to trace the origin of the products all the way back to their original source, to ensure that ethical and environmental aims and objectives are being met.

The impact of logistics and supply decisions

Logistics deals with coordinating the purchase and delivery of stocks of raw materials and finished goods, making sure suppliers deliver to the business and the business delivers to its customers. Decisions made by business operations will impact on a number of areas. These include:

Costs	The cost of stock and the cost of delivery impacts on the total cost of producing goods or supplying services. This in turn directly influences the price the customer is charged.
Reputation	The quality of the products and the customer service offered to the customer, such as delivery times, affects how the business is perceived. A business's reputation can be quickly damaged if products are of poor quality, faulty or not delivered on time.
Customer satisfaction	Customers are satisfied if the right products, of the right quality, are delivered on time. It is the role of logistics to make sure this happens. Satisfied customers promote businesses by word-of-mouth, especially on social media, whereas dissatisfied customers can damage a business's reputation, leading to a loss of repeat customers.

Key terms — Make sure you can write a definition for these key terms: bar gate stock graph, just in time (JIT), logistics, procurement

Retrieval

Answer the questions below. Cover the answers column with a piece of paper and write down as many answers as you can. Check and repeat.

Questions	Answers
1. What is a supplier?	A business that provides goods or services to another business
2. Why do some businesses hold buffer stock?	In case there are problems with stock deliveries
3. How is lead time calculated?	delivery date – date of order
4. What is JIT stock control?	A stock control system where stock is delivered just as it is needed; businesses using JIT do not hold buffer stock
5. State two advantages of using a JIT stock control system.	Two from: lower storage costs / less risk of damage to stock / no obsolete stock / less cash tied up in holding stock
6. State two disadvantages of a JIT stock control system.	Two from: need to handle more frequent deliveries / costs may be higher than buying in bulk / risk of running out of stock if deliveries are disrupted
7. What is meant by the term 'procurement'?	It is the process of identifying suitable suppliers and buying the necessary stock from them
8. Give the five criteria a business will consider when choosing its suppliers.	Quality; delivery (speed, reliability, cost); availability; cost; trust
9. If the prices paid by a business for the goods and services delivered are high, what might this mean for the customer?	Higher prices
10. What does logistics deal with?	Coordinating the purchase and delivery of stocks of raw materials and finished goods, making sure suppliers deliver to the business and the business delivers to its customers
11. State three impacts of logistics and supply decisions on businesses.	Costs; reputation; customer satisfaction

Previous questions

Use the questions below to check your knowledge from previous chapters.

Questions	Answers
1. What is an integrated marketing mix?	A marketing mix where each element works to support the other three
2. What is meant by the term 'business operations'?	The day-to-day activities of a business to meet its overall purpose
3. State two main purposes of business.	To produce goods; to provide services

30 Working with suppliers

Practice 30

Exam-style questions

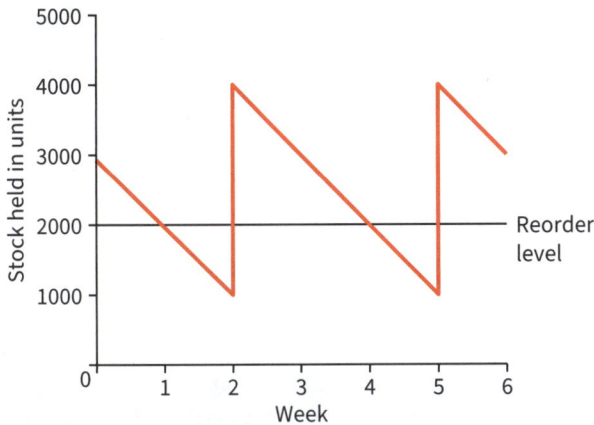

▲ **Figure 1** A bar gate stock graph

30.1 Using the data in Figure 1, calculate the lead time. **(1)**

EXAM TIP
When asked to calculate an answer, it is important to be accurate and express your answer using the correct unit of measurement; for example: units, %, weeks.

30.2 Using the data in Figure 1, calculate the reorder quantity. **(1)**

30.3 Explain *one* ethical consideration for a business when working with suppliers. **(3)**

30.4 Discuss the impact of logistics decisions on a business. **(6)**

Gothic Games is a leading manufacturer of hand-held game consoles, which are made and sold in the UK.

Kimico, the CEO, is keen to keep costs down. She imports major components, including chips and circuit boards, from abroad. Her main supplier, TechByte, offers a reliable service and quality products at a reasonable cost. Gothic Games uses a just in time stock control system, and Kimico has learned to trust her supplier. However, in 2021, disaster struck and TechByte was unable to source sufficient supplies of chips for Gothic Games to produce enough goods to meet the high demand over the Christmas period. Production stopped because Gothic Games did not have any spare chips in stock. This seriously damaged Gothic Games' reputation.

30.5 Outline *one* purpose of Gothic Games' business operations. **(2)**

30.6 Outline *one* consideration for Kimico when choosing suppliers. **(2)**

30.7 In order to improve customer satisfaction, Gothic Games is considering two options:

Option 1: continue with a just in time stock control system but source components in the UK

Option 2: move away from a just in time stock control system.

Justify which *one* of these two options Gothic Games should choose. **(9)**

Knowledge

31 Managing quality

Why is quality important?

Quality is achieved when goods and services meet customer expectations. Quality should be consistent.

Quality brings a range of benefits, including:

- customer satisfaction
- brand loyalty
- positive reviews on social media and by word of mouth
- less waste, because there is no need to offer refunds or scrap products
- motivated employees, who are proud of where they work and pleased not to be dealing with complaints.

Quality control and quality assurance

There are two methods of ensuring quality: **quality control** and **quality assurance**.

Quality control

Quality control is when quality is checked at the end of the production process before the finished product is delivered to customers.

Advantages and disadvantages

✓ Checking is carried out by a specialist inspector	✗ High levels of waste if a fault is found at the end of the production process
✓ Products are checked before being sent to the customer	✗ Need to employ a specialist inspector
✓ Does not increase the workload of production operatives	✗ Does not encourage production operatives to be personally responsible for quality

Quality assurance

Quality assurance is when quality is checked at every stage of the production process. Each production operative is responsible for checking the quality of their own work before passing the product to the next stage of the process.

Advantages and disadvantages

✓ Increases **motivation** because production operatives are given a sense of responsibility	✗ May reduce productivity because production operatives spend time checking their own work
✓ Reduces waste because faults are picked up early	✗ Increased training costs
✓ A focus on quality throughout the process	✗ Employees may feel overwhelmed

Controlling costs to gain a competitive advantage

Quality products help a business control costs. Less waste and fewer faulty products reduces the cost of raw materials, correcting mistakes, handling complaints and scrapping faulty products. Reduced costs can be passed onto the consumer in the form of lower prices, giving the business a competitive advantage.

Businesses also have a competitive advantage if they have a reputation for providing quality products that meet customer expectations.

 **Key terms** Make sure you can write a definition for these key terms

motivation   quality
quality assurance
quality control

31

Answer the questions below. Cover the answers column with a piece of paper and write down as many answers as you can. Check and repeat.

Questions | Answers

	Questions	Answers
1	When is quality achieved?	When goods and services meet customer expectations
2	State three reasons why quality is important.	Three from: customer satisfaction / brand loyalty / positive reviews on social media and by word of mouth / less waste / motivated employees
3	What is quality control?	Quality is checked at the end of the production process before the finished product is delivered to customers

Previous questions

Use the questions below to check your knowledge from previous chapters.

	Questions	Answers
1	State three different methods of production.	Job production; batch production; flow production
2	What is meant by the term 'procurement'?	It is the process of identifying suitable suppliers and buying the necessary stock from them

Exam-style questions

Jimini Toys plc manufactures a wide range of wooden toys using batch production. This ensures the retailers that stock its toys always have a good selection for customers to choose from. All toys are checked by an inspector before leaving the factory. Jimini Toys plc prides itself on making high-quality products that are safe for young children to play with. A puppet currently sells for £24.99.

Jimini Toys plc is seeing a fall in sales as customers switch to substantially cheaper wooden toys sold in discount supermarkets. Rian, the marketing director, thinks the prices of Jimini Toys plc's toys are too high. He has suggested to the operations director that the business moves to flow production to allow it to cut costs to lower prices while maintaining the current level of profit.

31.1 Outline *one* benefit to Jimini Toys plc of using quality control. (2)

31.2 Analyse the importance of quality to Jimini Toys plc. (6)

31.3 Evaluate whether Jimini Toys plc should change to flow production to give it a competitive advantage. You should use the information provided as well as your knowledge of business. (12)

Knowledge

32 The sales process

What is the sales process?

The **sales process** is the stages of interaction between a business and a customer, from initial enquiry through to final sale and beyond.

Effective communication between a business and its customers throughout the sales process leads to customer satisfaction and a better understanding of customer needs.

> **REVISION TIP**
>
> Think about the sales process as a continual flow, where each stage is dependent on the stage before.

Product knowledge
When a customer is interested in a product, they often want to talk to a well-informed member of the sales team. If this does not happen, they might go elsewhere and the business will lose the sale.

Post-sales service
After a sale has been completed, a business should try and maintain a relationship with its customers. This could include offering extended warranties, technical support and so on.

Speed and efficiency of service
Customers want to be served promptly. They also want to find products available to buy and be delivered within the expected time frame. If this does not happen, they might go elsewhere and the business will lose the sale.

Responses to customer feedback
It is important to respond to feedback from customers. Positive feedback should be acknowledged and, if appropriate, shared with the staff involved to motivate employees. Negative feedback should be addressed by acknowledging the customer's complaint and, if possible, offering to resolve the problem.

Customer engagement
Customers want a positive experience. This can include a good in-store atmosphere, a website that is easy to use, and attention from a sales person. If this does not happen, the customer might go elsewhere and the business will lose the sale.

The importance of providing good customer service

The sales process ensures that good customer service is provided. Customer service is meeting customer expectations before, during and after a sale. This can give a business a competitive advantage.

The benefits of good customer service include:

- customer loyalty
- a strong brand reputation
- a reduction in negative publicity
- motivated employees
- an increase in market share
- increased profitability.

Key terms — Make sure you can write a definition for this key term

sales process

Retrieval 32

Answer the questions below. Cover the answers column with a piece of paper and write down as many answers as you can. Check and repeat.

Questions | Answers

1 What are the five stages of the sales process? | Product knowledge; speed and efficiency of service; customer engagement; responses to customer feedback; post-sales service

2 Give two examples of post-sales service. | Extended warranties; technical support

3 What is good customer service? | Meeting or exceeding customer expectations before, during and after a sale

4 Give two benefits of good customer service. | Two from: customer loyalty / a strong brand reputation / a reduction in negative publicity / motivated employees / an increase in market share / increased profitability

Previous questions

Use the questions below to check your knowledge from previous chapters.

Questions | Answers

1 Give the five criteria a business will consider when choosing its suppliers. | Quality; delivery (speed, reliability, cost); availability; cost; trust

2 When is quality achieved? | When goods and services meet customers' expectations

Practice

Exam-style questions

32.1 Which *one* of the following is a benefit of good customer service? (1)

    A Product knowledge   C Post-sales service

    B Strong brand reputation   D Understanding customer needs

32.2 Explain *one* benefit to a business of using technology in promotion. (3)

32.3 Discuss the impact on a business of providing good customer service. (6)

Practice

Exam-style questions

Lotus Leisure plc manufactures and sells high-quality yoga and Pilates clothing, including leggings and t-shirts. It makes each product in a wide range of colours and sizes.

Lotus Leisure plc's target market is women with high levels of disposable income. It only sells its products through its own e-commerce site, and promotes them via fashion magazines. It charges a high price; typically, 5% above other leading brands such as Lululemon.

The operations department uses a quality control system, and all the clothes are produced using batch production. They are made by low- to medium-skilled workers, and batches move from the cutting room to the sewing machines, before being tested and packaged.

Lotus Leisure plc prides itself on offering excellent customer service, with a dedicated telephone help line that is open from 7 a.m. to 8 p.m. six days a week.

In recent months, the helpline has experienced a large increase in the number of calls it receives. Customers are all making the same complaint: the quality of the material used to make the clothes they have just bought is not the quality they are used to. There has also been an increase in negative comments on social media.

32.4 State *one* good that Lotus Leisure plc produces in its factories. **(1)**

32.5 Define the term 'quality'. **(1)**

32.6 Outline *one* benefit to Lotus Leisure plc of selling high-quality clothes. **(2)**

> **EXAM TIP**
> When answering an 'Analyse' question, look for information in the case study that links to the business term in the question. This question is about market segmentation, so you should include the market segment that Lotus Leisure plc is targeting in your answer: women who have high levels of disposable income.

32.7 Analyse the impact on Lotus Leisure plc of using market segmentation. **(6)**

32.8 In order to improve its competitive advantage, Lotus Leisure plc is considering two options.

Option 1: introduce a quality assurance system

Option 2: change to flow production.

Justify which *one* of these two options Lotus Leisure plc should choose. **(9)**

> **EXAM TIP**
> Do not confuse quality assurance and quality control. Think AbC. A for assurance starts at the beginning of the process, C for control comes at the end of the process.

32.9 Evaluate the importance of post-sales service to Lotus Leisure plc in maintaining a reputation for quality. You should use the information provided as well as your knowledge of business. **(12)**

32 Practice

Knowledge

33 Business calculations

Gross and net profit

Gross profit is the profit left after the cost of sales has been deducted from sales revenue.

Net profit is the profit left after all other expenses have been deducted from the gross profit.

(sales) revenue = price × quantity

gross profit = sales revenue − cost of sales

net profit = gross profit − other operating expenses and interest

LINK

You were introduced to sales revenue in Chapter 1 and cost of sales in Chapter 8. If you need to, revisit these chapters to check your understanding of these terms.

EXAM TIP

In your exams, you might find 'revenue', 'sales revenue' and even 'total revenue' used interchangeably.

Example calculations of gross profit and net profit

	£000s	Explanation
Sales revenue	950	Income coming into the business from sales
Cost of sales	325	The direct cost of producing the goods or services sold
Gross profit	625	sales revenue − cost of sales 950 − 325 = 625
Other expenses and interest	480	The sum of all other expenses, including heat and light, wages and salaries, marketing and distribution
Net profit	145	gross profit − other expenses and interest 625 − 480 = 145

Remember, a business may make a loss. In the example above, let's assume that other expenses and interest is actually £650,000. What happens to the net profit? When the figure is negative, it is shown in brackets: (25).

	£000s	Explanation
Gross profit	625	
Other expenses and interest	650	
Net profit	(25)	gross profit − other expenses and interest 625 − 650 = (25)

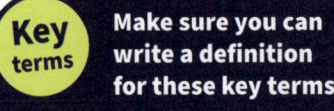

Make sure you can write a definition for these key terms

average rate of return   gross profit margin   net profit margin

Profit margins

Gross and net profit calculations help a business understand how profit is being generated and whether costs are too high or not.

However, profit margins are a better measure of a business's profitability (a business's ability to generate profit from sales made), and they enable better comparisons of profitability over time and between businesses.

gross profit margin (%) = $\dfrac{\text{gross profit}}{\text{sales revenue}} \times 100$

net profit margin (%) = $\dfrac{\text{net profit}}{\text{sales revenue}} \times 100$

Example calculations of gross profit margin and net profit margin

Example 1

		Explanation
Sales revenue	£950,000	
Gross profit	£625,000	
Gross profit margin	$\dfrac{625{,}000}{950{,}000} \times 100 = 65.79\%$	65.79% of sales revenue is maintained as gross profit. This means that for every £100 made in sales, £65.79 is gross profit. If this figure is falling, it may imply that the cost of sales is not being managed effectively or that suppliers are increasing their prices. If this happens, a business may look to reduce waste or find new suppliers.

Example 2

		Explanation
Sales revenue	£950,000	
Net profit	£145,000	
Net profit margin	$\dfrac{145{,}000}{950{,}000} \times 100 = 15.26\%$	15.26% of sales revenue is maintained as net profit. This means that for every £100 made in sales, £15.26 is net profit. If this figure is falling, assuming gross profit margin is relatively unchanged, it may imply that operating expenses are not being managed effectively. A business may look to reduce their utility bills or review the number of people it employs.

Knowledge

33 Business calculations

Average rate of return

Businesses make decisions about investments. For example, they decide whether or not it is worthwhile to buy a new machine, open a new shop or take over a competitor. The directors of a public limited company may have to justify such decisions to shareholders.

One calculation used to weigh up the financial benefit of an investment or to compare investment options is **average rate of return** (ARR). This is the average annual return on an investment as a percentage of the amount invested.

$$\text{average rate of return} = \frac{\text{average annual profit (total profit/number of years)}}{\text{cost of investment}} \times 100$$

Example calculation of average rate of return

The following data applies to a business considering investing in a new machine.

Cost of investment	Profit year 1	Profit year 2	Profit year 3
£1,200,000	£400,000	£600,000	£600,000

		Explanation
Average annual profit	£500,000	The sum of the profit for year 1, year 2 and year 3, divided by the number of years $$\frac{400{,}000 + 600{,}000 + 600{,}000}{3} = £500{,}000$$
Cost of investment	£1,200,000	The amount spent or to be spent on buying the investment (on buying the new machine)
Average rate of return	41.67%	$\frac{\text{average annual profit}}{\text{cost of investment}} \times 100$ $\frac{500{,}000}{1{,}200{,}000} \times 100 = 41.67\%$ An ARR of 41.67% means that, for every £100 invested, the business generates on average an additional annual profit of £41.67.

If a business is comparing two or more investment opportunities then, based purely on numbers, it would go with the investment with the highest ARR because this is the investment that is forecast to give the business the highest annual return.

However, a business may not make a decision purely on numbers. It may consider other factors such as risk, ethics, and the environmental impact of the investment.

> **REVISION TIP**
>
> Summarise all of the formulas in this chapter on one sheet of A3 paper. Remember gross profit and net profit should be shown as £s, whereas gross profit margin, net profit margin, and ARR are always expressed as a percentage.

Retrieval 33

Answer the questions below. Cover the answers column with a piece of paper and write down as many answers as you can. Check and repeat.

Questions / Answers

#	Question	Answer
1	What is the formula for gross profit?	gross profit = sales revenue − cost of sales
2	What is meant by the term 'cost of sales'?	The direct cost of producing the goods or services sold
3	What is the formula for net profit?	net profit = gross profit − other operating expenses and interest
4	Give two examples of a business's expenses.	Two from: heat and light / wages and salaries / marketing / distribution
5	What is the formula for gross profit margin?	$\text{gross profit margin (\%)} = \dfrac{\text{gross profit}}{\text{sales revenue}} \times 100$
6	What is the formula for net profit margin?	$\text{net profit margin (\%)} = \dfrac{\text{net profit}}{\text{sales revenue}} \times 100$
7	What is meant by the term 'average rate of return (ARR)'?	The average annual return on an investment as a percentage of the amount invested
8	What is the formula for ARR?	$= \dfrac{\text{average annual profit (total profit/number of years)}}{\text{cost of investment}} \times 100$
9	If you are comparing two investment opportunities, would a business normally choose the one with the highest ARR or the lowest ARR?	The one with the highest ARR
10	State one non-numeric factor a business may take into account when making an investment decision.	One from: risk / ethics / the environmental impact of the investment

Previous questions

Use the questions below to check your knowledge from previous chapters.

Questions / Answers

#	Question	Answer
1	What is the formula for calculating revenue?	(sales) revenue = price × quantity
2	What is the difference between a merger and a takeover?	A merger is when two or more businesses agree to join together to operate as one. A takeover is when one business buys a second business
3	What are the five stages of the sales process?	Product knowledge; speed and efficiency of service; customer engagement; responses to customer feedback; post-sales service

Practice

Exam-style questions

33.1 Table 1 shows the financial performance of a business.

	£ millions
Sales revenue	25.5
Cost of sales	12
Gross profit	13.4
Other expenses and interest	8.2

▲ **Table 1**

Using the information in Table 1, calculate the business's net profit. You are advised to show your workings. **(2)**

33.2 Using the information in Table 1, calculate the business's gross profit margin to two decimal places. You are advised to show your workings. **(2)**

33.3 Discuss the impact on a business of a falling net profit margin. **(6)**

> **EXAM TIP**
>
> 'Calculate' questions may ask you to give your answer to two decimal places. This means you need two numbers after the decimal point; for example, 29.92%. If the third number after the decimal point is a 5 or above, you should round up: 2.56542% to two decimal places is 2.57%. If the third number after the decimal point is a 4 or lower, you should ignore it: 16.4932% to two decimal places is 16.49%.

Keep Moving plc is a manufacturing business that produces mobility aids, such as wheelchairs and walking frames. It prides itself on offering a wide range of products at affordable prices. However, costs have started to increase leading to a fall in Keep Moving plc's profitability. Seth, the managing director, wants to keep manufacturing in the UK so is looking at ways to lower costs by introducing more machinery into the factory. This would lead to 30% of production operatives losing their jobs.

	2024 (£000s)	2023 (£000s)
Sales revenue		3800
Cost of sales	1980	1200
Gross profit	1400	2600
Net profit	(120)	900

▲ **Table 2** Keep Moving plc's financial performance in 2023 and 2024

Average annual profit	£230,000
Cost of investment	£1,000,000

▲ **Table 3** Information about a new piece of machinery that Keep Moving plc wants to purchase

33.4 Using the information in Table 2, calculate Keep Moving plc's sales revenue in 2024. You are advised to show your workings. **(2)**

33.5 Using the information in Table 2, calculate Keep Moving plc's other operating expenses and interest in 2024. You are advised to show your workings. **(2)**

33.6 Using the information in Table 2, calculate Keep Moving plc's net profit margin in 2023 to two decimal places. You are advised to show your workings. **(2)**

33.7 Using the information in Table 3, calculate the average rate of return to two decimal places. You are advised to show your workings. **(2)**

33.8 Outline *one* external source of finance Keep Moving plc could use to finance the new machinery. **(2)**

33.9 Analyse the impact on Keep Moving plc if Seth decides to invest in new machinery for the factory. **(6)**

Knowledge

33 Understanding business performance

Using and interpreting quantitative business data

Quantitative business data is numerical information about a business or the market in which it operates.

Businesses have access to a large amount of external data (such as market trends) and internal data (such as monthly sales). This quantitative data is used to support, inform and justify business decisions, such as whether to enter or exit a market.

Information from graphs and charts

Graphs and charts provide businesses with a visual summary of quantitative data, making it easier to interpret the data and spot trends; for example, fluctuations in share values over time or a comparison of monthly sales of two competing businesses.

Graphs and charts include bar charts, pie charts, and line graphs.

Bar charts

Bar charts show categories on the *x*-axis and frequency on the *y*-axis.

In this bar chart, 28% of respondents to a survey said that their preferred colour of car was white.

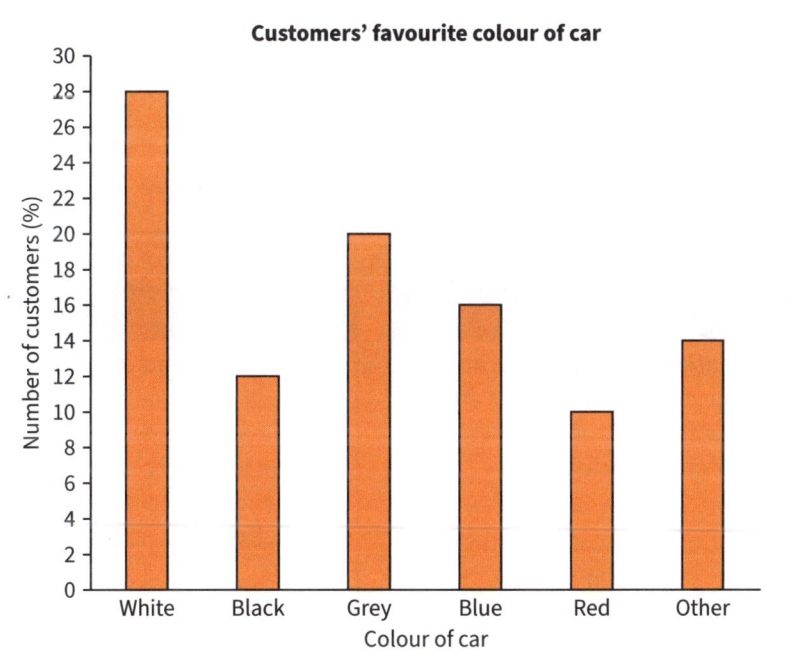

> **REVISION TIP**
>
> Look at past papers to see the range of graphs and charts used. It is important, when interpreting graphs and charts, to read the title and the labels on the axes carefully.

> **REVISION TIP**
>
> You will not be asked to draw a graph or a chart in your exams. You may, however, be asked to interpret one, or answer a calculation question using data presented as a chart or graph.

Knowledge

34 Understanding business performance

Pie charts

A pie chart shows data as a percentage of a whole. The size of each portion of the pie chart represents the percentage of the whole.

In this pie chart, Business C is the market leader with 45% market share.

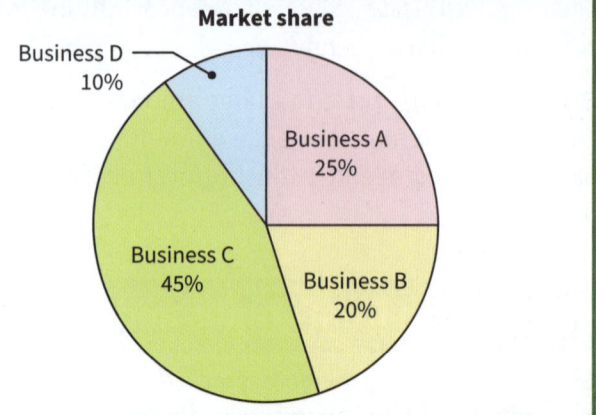

Line graphs

A line graph shows data at specific points over a period of time, to identify fluctuations and trends.

In this line graph, there are fluctuations in the business's share price, with a peak in Y1Q1 when the share price is £1.40, and a low in Y2Q2 when the share price is £0.90.

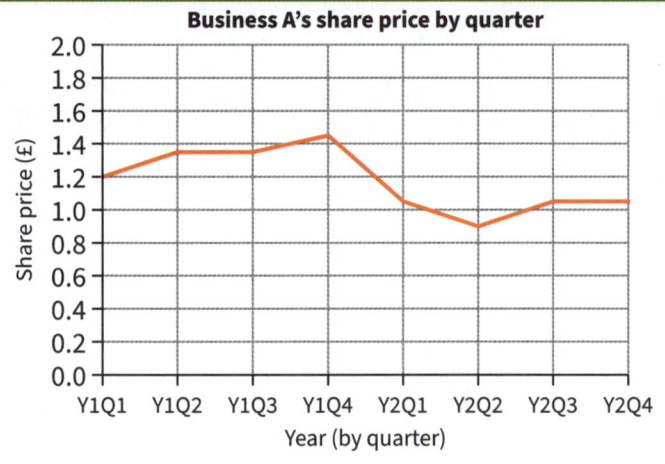

Financial data

Financial data is data about the financial performance of a business. Examples include:
- gross profit and net profit by product, branch, or over time
- gross profit margin and net profit margin on an annual basis
- fluctuations in costs of raw materials
- average rate of return
- annual sales revenue.

Marketing data

Marketing data is data about the marketing activities and performance of a business. Examples include:
- expenditure on advertising
- trends in followers on social media
- response to a product trial or a special offer
- sales before and after a change in price.

Market data

Market data is data about the market or industry as a whole. Analysing market data allows a business to compare its performance to the performance of its competitors, and enables it to identify trends. Examples include:
- average household expenditure
- sales of each business operating in the market
- number of imports and exports
- growth or decline in industry revenue over time.

The use and limitations of financial data

Financial data can be used to understand business performance.

Uses	Limitations
• Gross and net profit can be analysed to see how a business is performing over time. • Gross and net profit margins can be analysed to see how efficient the business is at generating profit from sales. • Actual average rate of return on an investment can be compared to the forecasted average rate of return. • Comparisons can be made with other businesses operating in the same market.	• Financial data only provides quantitative information. It cannot provide information about other factors, such as ethical sourcing of raw materials. • It does not provide reasons for fluctuations in financial performance, such as a one-off order resulting in above-average sales in the first quarter of the year. • Financial performance might be influenced by factors outside a business's control, such as rising interest rates, so it is unfair to judge employees' performance on financial data alone.

Financial data can also be used to make business decisions.

Uses	Limitations
• Average rate of return can be calculated to choose between investment opportunities. • Profit margins can be analysed to find out if costs are too high, and looking at individual costs may indicate changes that can be made to lower costs, such as changing suppliers. • Sales data can be analysed to make decisions on individual products; for example, whether to let a product go into decline or invest in an extension strategy. • Sales data can be analysed to compare sales at different stores within a business.	• Past data is not always a fair indication of the future, so decisions based only on financial data may be ill-informed. • Quantitative data does not illustrate qualitative factors, such as the impact of a decision on staff motivation. • Data is open to interpretation and a manager may be biased in the way they interpret results. • Data can be manipulated and a manager may use data to make a decision that is more favourable to their department than the business as a whole.

Key terms — Make sure you can write a definition for these key terms

financial data   market data   marketing data

Retrieval

Answer the questions below. Cover the answers column with a piece of paper and write down as many answers as you can. Check and repeat.

Questions / Answers

#	Question	Answer
1	What is quantitative business data?	Numerical information about a business or the market in which it operates
2	How does a business use quantitative data?	To support, inform and justify business decisions
3	Graphs and charts provide businesses with what? Why?	A visual summary of quantitative data, which makes it easier to interpret and spot trends
4	Name three types of charts or graphs a business may use.	Bar charts; pie charts; line graphs
5	What do bar charts show on the *x*-axis and on the *y*-axis?	Categories on the *x*-axis and frequency on the *y*-axis
6	What does a pie chart show?	Data as a percentage of a whole
7	What does a line graph show?	Data at specific points over a period of time, to identify fluctuations and trends
8	Give two examples of financial data a business may use when making business decisions.	Two from: gross profit and net profit by product, branch, or over time / gross profit margin and net profit margin on an annual basis / fluctuations in costs of raw materials / average rate of return / annual sales revenue
9	Give two examples of marketing data a business may use when making business decisions.	Two from: expenditure on advertising / trends in followers on social media / response to a product trial or a special offer / sales in comparison with a change in price
10	Give two examples of market data a business may use when making business decisions.	Two from: average household expenditure / sales of each business operating in the market / number of imports and exports / growth in industry revenue over time

Previous questions

Use the questions below to check your knowledge from previous chapters.

#	Question	Answer
1	What is good customer service?	Meeting or exceeding customer expectations before, during and after a sale
2	What is the formula for net profit margin?	$\text{net profit margin (\%)} = \dfrac{\text{net profit}}{\text{sales revenue}} \times 100$
3	What is meant by the term 'average rate of return (ARR)'?	The average annual return on an investment as a percentage of the amount invested

34 Understanding business performance

Practice

Exam-style questions

34.1 Table 1 shows the sales revenue of four businesses operating in a market in 2023 and 2024.

	2023 (£000s)	2024 (£000s)
Businesses A	750	725
Businesses B	650	650
Businesses C	980	1005
Businesses D	340	330

▲ Table 1

Using the information in Table 1, calculate the market share of the top two businesses in 2024 to two decimal places. You are advised to show your workings. **(2)**

EXAM TIP

Market share is the percentage of the total market that a business occupies. You calculate a business's market share by first calculating the total market, and then working out the business's market as a percentage of the total market.

34.2 Using the information in Table 1, calculate the percentage growth or decline in the market from 2023 to 2024 to two decimal places. You are advised to show your workings. **(2)**

34.3 Table 2 shows the financial performance of a business.

	£ millions
Sales revenue	8.2
Gross profit	4.8
Other expenses and interest	2.3
Net profit	1.1

▲ Table 2

Using the information in Table 2, calculate the business's net profit margin to two decimal places. **(2)**

34.4 Explain *one* benefit to a business of using charts and graphs to show marketing data. **(3)**

34.5 Discuss the importance to a business of using quantitative business data in decision-making. **(6)**

Exam-style questions

Regency Coach Tours plc is an established business offering coach tours across England, Wales, and Scotland. The coach tours vary from three days to one week, and customers are normally taken to places of interest such as castles and stately homes. Regency Coach Tours plc uses hotels owned by recognised chains, such as Hilton® and Holiday Inn®, and the average age of its customers is 68 years old.

Julietta Spencer, the managing director, is keen to grow the business through organic growth. The business currently has a fleet of 50 54-seat coaches and employs over 75 experienced drivers and 80 tour guides. Julietta thinks that Regency Coach Tours plc should invest in four more 54-seat coaches, which cost £205,000 each.

Julietta's son, Conrad, the marketing director, has looked at trends in the market and has identified that the UK has an ageing population. Conrad thinks Regency Coach Tours plc should buy ten smaller, 29-seat coaches to offer one- or two-day trips. He believes that these shorter trips will appeal to a slightly older demographic, to people over 75 years old. These smaller coaches could then also be used for private hire, such as weddings.

Cost of a 29-seat coach	£120,000
Number of years in the business	6 years
Annual profit	£40,000

▲ **Table 1** *Cost and forecast profit for a 29-seat coach*

The business's financial performance over the last four years has been good with an average annual net profit of £3 million. However, profit is difficult to predict because petrol prices fluctuate regularly and account for 33% of total costs.

34.6 Define the term 'organic growth'. (1)

> **EXAM TIP**
> Keep definitions short and precise, and try not to repeat the term in your definition. What does 'organic' mean? What does 'growth' mean?

34.7 Outline *one* way in which Regency Coach Tours plc uses market data. (2)

34.8 Using the information in Table 1, calculate the average rate of return for a 29-seat coach to two decimal places. You are advised to show your workings. (2)

34.9 Analyse the impact on Regency Coach Tours plc of using financial data to measure business performance. (6)

34.10 In order to achieve growth, Regency Coach Tours plc is considering two options:

Option 1: invest in ten 29-seat coaches, and offer one- and two-day trips

Option 2: invest in an additional four 54-seat coaches, and run more existing tours.

Justify which *one* of these two options Regency Coach Tours plc should choose. (9)

> **EXAM TIP**
> Look for evidence in the case study of arguments for and against both options before making a decision about which option you think the business should choose. Decide which option you are going to recommend before you start writing. Will it be ten smaller coaches or four larger coaches? Use numbers to support your argument, such as the average rate of return for both options.

34.11 Evaluate the importance of financial data in making a decision about how to best grow Regency Coach Tours plc. You should use the information provided as well as your knowledge of business. (12)

34 Practice

Knowledge

35 Organisational structure

Organisational structures

A business's organisational structure sets out how employees are organised in terms of who reports to whom. The nature of the organisational structure determines:

- the **chain of command**: how communication flows through the hierarchy
- the **span of control**: the number of employees each manager is directly responsible for.

An organisation chart is a diagram that shows each employee's position in the hierarchy.

An organisational structure can be:

- hierarchical or flat
- centralised or decentralised.

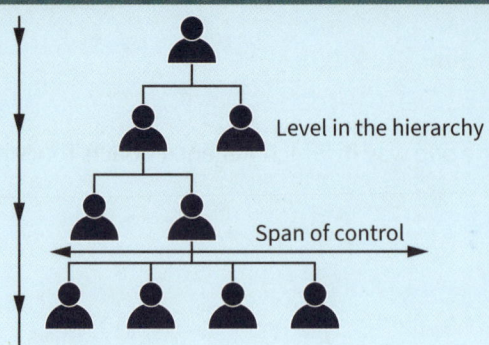

Chain of command
▲ An organisational structure

> **REVISION TIP**
>
> A common mistake students often make is thinking that 'span of control' is all the employees who report to a manager, rather than those who report *directly* to a manager. For example, all the staff at your school or college ultimately report to the head teacher, but only a small number of people report directly to the head teacher.

Hierarchical organisational structures

Characteristics of **hierarchical organisational structures** include:

- many levels in the organisational structure
- a long chain of command
- each manager has a narrow span of control.

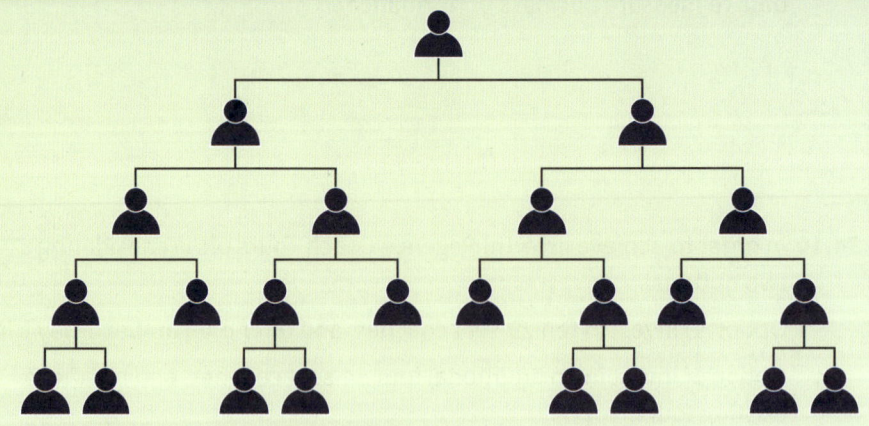

▲ A hierarchical organisational structure

Flat organisational structures

Characteristics of **flat organisational structures** include:

- few levels in the organisational structure
- a short chain of command
- each manager has a wide span of control.

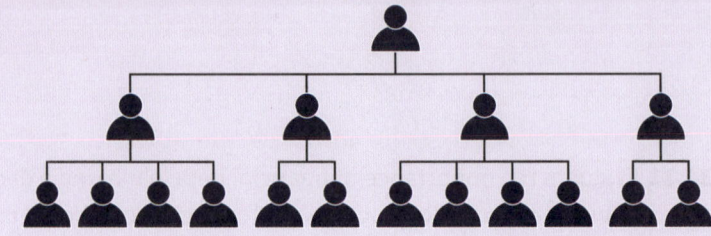

▲ A flat organisational structure

Centralised organisational structures

In a **centralised organisational structure**, decisions are made by a few managers at the top of the hierarchy. These decisions are then passed down the hierarchy. This means that decisions are only being made by senior, more experienced employees or the owners.

Centralised organisation structure	
Advantages and disadvantages	
✔ Decisions made by senior members of staff	✘ Middle and junior managers may feel demotivated due to a lack of responsibility
✔ Greater consistency and control in decision-making	✘ The people making the decisions may be distant from the day-to-day operations of the business, and from employees and consumers
✔ Decisions are clearly focussed on the business aims and objectives	

Decentralised organisational structures

In a **decentralised organisational structure**, decision-making is delegated to managers throughout the hierarchy.

Decentralised organisation structure	
Advantages and disadvantages	
✔ More motivated middle and junior managers, who feel they are trusted to make decisions	✘ Decision-makers may be biased towards their own needs rather than the business's aims and objectives
✔ Decisions are made by people closer to the day-to-day operations of the business	✘ Middle and junior managers may lack experience
✔ Decisions can be implemented more quickly	✘ Greater risk of conflict between decision-makers

When are different organisational structures appropriate?

The appropriateness of different organisational structures depends on a range of factors. For example, how skilled are the workers?

- A skilled workforce may need less supervision and can be given more **autonomy** in decision-making, making a flat, decentralised organisational structure appropriate.
- If the workplace is highly automated, one supervisor may have a wide span of control, leading to a flat centralised organisational structure.

As businesses grow, the structure can become more complicated. For example, a business that has a lot of products or operates in more than one country may require a hierarchical structure.

Knowledge

35 Organisational structure

Why is effective communication important?

Effective communication means the correct message is received by the correct person, on time, and in a way that is understood. Effective communication helps ensure:

- employees understand their jobs
- employees are informed about what is happening in the business
- business aims and objectives are understood by everyone
- the business operates efficiently on a day-to-day basis
- the business delivers a high level of customer service.

Insufficient communication

Too little communication has an impact on efficiency, because employees do not have all the information they need to do their jobs properly.

Too little communication also has an impact on motivation, because employees feel they are not informed about what is going on in the business. A feeling of 'them and us' may develop, if workers feel managers are keeping information from them.

Inefficiency and a demotivated workforce lead to mistakes, quality falling, and poor customer service.

Excessive communication

Too much information has an impact on efficiency, because messages may be missed or misunderstood, and employees may waste time engaging with information that is not relevant to them.

Too much information also has an impact on motivation, because employees suffer from information overload, and can feel overwhelmed and confused.

Inefficiency and a demotivated workforce lead to mistakes, quality falling, and poor customer service.

Barriers to effective communication

A barrier is an obstacle that stops a message being received or understood by the recipient.

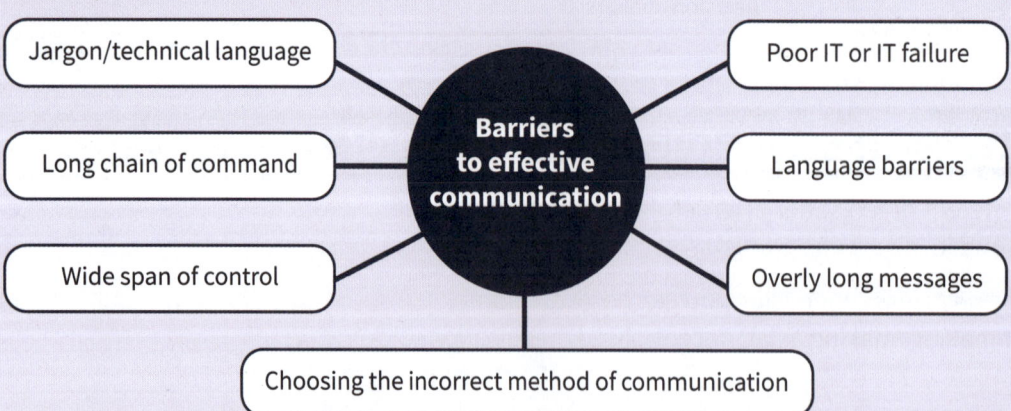

Barriers to effective communication:
- Jargon/technical language
- Long chain of command
- Wide span of control
- Poor IT or IT failure
- Language barriers
- Overly long messages
- Choosing the incorrect method of communication

Key terms — Make sure you can write a definition for these key terms: autonomy, centralised organisational structure, chain of command, decentralised organisational structure, flat organisational structure, hierarchical organisational structure, span of control

Different ways of working

Ways of working differ to suit both the business and the employees.

Full time	Employees are contracted to work 35 hours or more per week.
	This increases the employee's job security, and the employee may be more committed to their role as a result. However, it reduces flexibility for both the employer and the employee.
Part time	Employees are contracted to work less than 35 hours per week.
	This gives both the employer and the employee greater flexibility. It allows the employee to work alongside other commitments, such as caring for members of their family or studying.
Flexible hours	Employees may be given a set number of hours to work, such as 35 hours per week, but have the flexibility to choose when they work; for example, they might be able to choose a start time between 8:00am and 11:00am.
	Employers may retain the right to change the number of hours an employee works each week. This gives the employer greater flexibility, allowing them to match the hours worked with demand.
Permanent contracts	Employees are contracted to work indefinitely (the contract does not have an end date).
	Both the employer and the employee are more committed to each other. There is likely to be more training and opportunities for progression, leading to greater efficiency and motivation.
Temporary contracts	Employees are contracted to work for a set period of time; for example, for six months to cover maternity leave or for 12 months to work on a specific project.
	The employee helps to meet the short-term needs of the business. Although the employee does not have the security of a permanent contract, this can suit their needs.
	Sometimes a temporary contract can become a permanent contract.
Freelance contracts	Freelance workers are normally self-employed, offering their services to a range of different businesses and agreeing to task-based contracts.
	This allows a business to employ a specialist as and when needed, and it allows the freelancer to choose the contracts that interest them, and fit with their other work and personal commitments.

The impact of technology on ways of working

Technology impacts on many aspects of the way we work, from how we communicate, to how we produce goods and services, and even to where we work.

Technology has increased efficiency

Advances in technology have increased efficiency. For example:
- Many tasks originally carried out by employees are now carried out fully or partly by technology. For example, machinery is often used in production processes to increase productivity and achieve greater consistency in the quality of goods and services produced.
- Communication is now easier and quicker. Meetings can be held online using video conferencing software, reducing the need to travel, and files can be shared online and stored in the cloud.

Technology has enabled remote working

Technology has made it possible for some employees to work from anywhere, rather than always having to go into the office. This reduces costs for businesses (who can rent smaller premises and pay lower utility bills) and for employees (who no longer have to pay to travel to work every day).

Being able to work from home has led to greater flexibility and higher motivation for employees, who spend less time travelling. However, businesses can find it hard to supervise remote employees, and many argue teamwork suffers. If employees are distracted by working at home, there may also be a loss of productivity.

Retrieval

Answer the questions below. Cover the answers column with a piece of paper and write down as many answers as you can. Check and repeat.

	Questions	Answers
1	What is a business's organisational structure?	How employees are organised in terms of who reports to whom
2	State three characteristics of an hierarchical organisational structure.	Many levels in the organisational structure; long chain of command; each manager has a narrow span of control
3	State three characteristics of a flat organisational structure.	Few levels in the organisational structure; short chain of command; each manager has a wide span of control
4	What is the difference between a centralised and a decentralised organisational structure?	In a centralised organisational structure, decisions are made by a few managers at the top of the hierarchy. In a decentralised organisational structure, decisions are delegated to managers throughout the hierarchy
5	Give one example of when a flat, decentralised organisational structure is appropriate.	When the business has a skilled workforce that needs less supervision and can be given more autonomy in decision-making
6	Define 'effective communication'?	The correct message is received by the correct person, on time, and in a way that is understood
7	State two impacts of insufficient communication.	Inefficiency; a demotivated workforce
8	What is the difference between a permanent contract and a temporary contract?	With a permanent contract, an employee is contracted to work indefinitely. With a temporary contract, an employee is contracted to work for a set period of time
9	What are freelance contracts?	Task-based contracts
10	State two ways that technology has impacted on ways of working.	It has increased efficiency; it has enabled remote working

Previous questions

Use the questions below to check your knowledge from previous chapters.

	Questions	Answers
1	Give two examples of post-sales service.	Extended warranties; technical support
2	What is the formula for gross profit?	gross profit = sales revenue − cost of sales
3	Graphs and charts provide businesses with what? Why?	A visual summary of quantitative data, which makes it easier to interpret and spot trends

35 Organisational structure

Practice 35

Exam-style questions

35.1 Which *one* of the following is a defining characteristic of a centralised organisational structure? **(1)**

- **A** Short chain of command
- **B** Many levels in the hierarchy
- **C** Effective communication
- **D** Decisions made by a few at the top of the hierarchy

35.2 Which *two* of the following are examples of marketing data? **(2)**

- **A** Number of businesses competing
- **B** Gross profit margin
- **C** Trends in followers on social media
- **D** Expenditure on advertising
- **E** Average household expenditure

35.3 Explain *one* impact of excessive communication in a business. **(3)**

35.4 Discuss the impact on a business of decentralised decision-making. **(6)**

Central Calls plc provides call centre support to other large businesses including e-tailers, banks and energy companies. Rather than each business having a team of people who talk to customers, all calls are answered by Central Calls plc.

Central Calls plc operates 24 hours a day, 7 days a week, 365 days per year. It employs over 1000 telephone operatives who work from a large office on the outskirts of London. When Central Calls plc first opened, it faced very little competition. However, in recent years, the market has become increasingly competitive, with call centres operating abroad undercutting Central Calls plc on price. Central Calls plc is also finding it increasingly difficult to attract new employees.

Central Calls plc has decided to allow employees to work from home. To make this work they need to upgrade their IT system. Central Calls plc has a centralised organisational structure and the Managing Director, Sajid, has suggested that they employ the services of a freelance specialist to upgrade the system and to train employees on how to operate it from home.

35.5 Define 'public limited company (plc)'. **(1)**

35.6 Outline *one* benefit to Central Calls plc of having a centralised organisational structure. **(2)**

35.7 Analyse the impact on Central Calls plc of using a freelance specialist to upgrade the IT system and train employees. **(6)**

35.8 Evaluate the impact on Central Calls plc of introducing remote working for its telephone operatives. You should use the information provided as well as your knowledge of business. **(12)**

> **EXAM TIP**
>
> 'Analyse' questions must be answered in context. This means using information from the case study in your answer. For example, when thinking about the impact of using a freelance specialist to train staff, consider that Central Calls plc has over 1000 employees.

Knowledge

36 Effective recruitment

Job roles and responsibilities

Every employee has an employment contract that outlines their **job role**. A job role is an employee's position within an organisational structure, and it determines their responsibilities and the tasks they complete at work.

> **REVISION TIP**
>
> When revising job roles and responsibilities, practise linking this information to different organisational structures to consider how responsibilities might vary between businesses. For example, how does the role of a senior manager differ in a centralised organisational structure and a decentralised organisational structure?

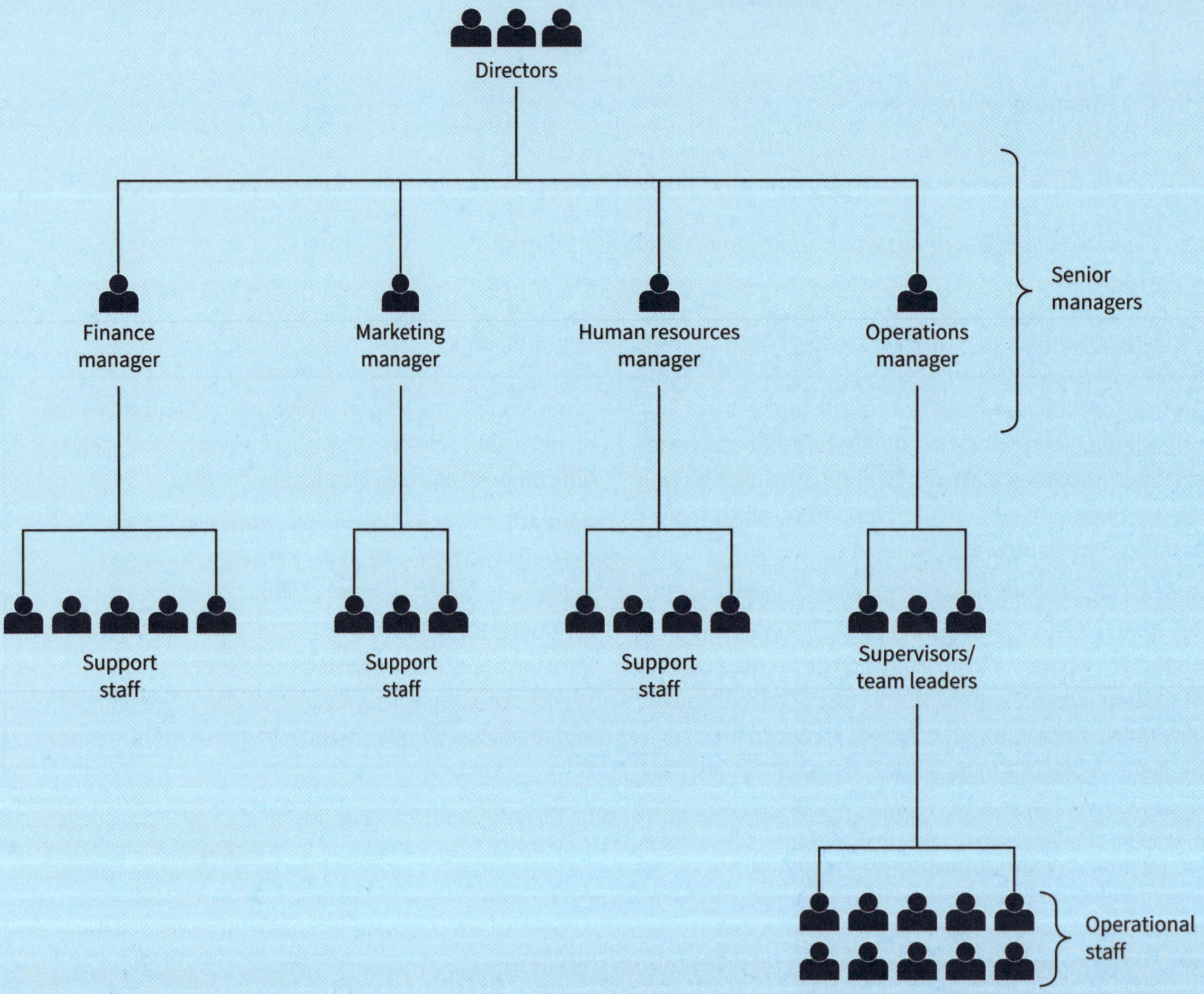

▲ A diagram showing how employees fit into an organisational structure based on their job role

Directors
- The top level of the organisational structure.
- As a group, they form the board of directors.
- Responsible for ensuring the business meets its aims and objectives.
- Responsible for medium- to long-term decision-making.
- Responsible for ensuring the business meets its statutory responsibilities, including paying taxes and filing company accounts.
- The managing director oversees the whole business, while other directors have responsibility for specific functions; for example, the finance director.

Senior managers
- Towards the top of the hierarchy.
- Report to a director; for example, the marketing manager reports to the marketing director.
- Responsible for the day-to-day running of a business function; for example, human resources.
- Responsible for managing a group of employees. Depending on the size of the business, and the organisational structure, this could be junior managers or support staff.

Supervisors/team leaders
- In the middle of the hierarchy.
- Report to senior manager, normally the operations manager.
- Responsible for overseeing the day-to-day production of goods or services.
- Responsible for ensuring quality.
- Responsible for managing a group of employees, usually operational staff.

Operational staff and support staff
- Towards the bottom of the hierarchy.
- Report to senior managers, junior managers or supervisors/team leaders, depending on the organisational structure.
- Office-based staff tend to be called support staff; for example, a human resources assistant or a marketing apprentice.
- Factory-based staff tend to be called operational staff; for example, a production operative making components on a production line.
- Have little or no supervisory responsibilities.

Knowledge

36 Effective recruitment

How do businesses recruit employees?

The **recruitment process** is the steps taken to attract suitable candidates to apply for a job vacancy. As part of the recruitment process, businesses produce two key documents:

- **person specification**
- **job description**.

These documents are used to inform a job advertisement to attract applicants, and also as part of the **selection process**. The selection process involves shortlisting suitable candidates and inviting them to attend an interview.

Once a vacancy has been advertised, applicants will be asked to complete an application form and/or submit a **curriculum vitae (CV)**.

> **REMEMBER**
>
> Do not confuse a person specification and a job description. The big clue is in the name. The person specification is about the type of person the business wants to recruit. The job description is about the job role that the successful candidate will be appointed to.

Person specification
A person specification outlines the qualifications, skills, experience, and characteristics the business is looking for in a successful candidate.

Each category may be split into essential (must have) requirements and desirable (would be nice to have) requirements.

Job description
A job description outlines the job role and the responsibilities associated with it.

It includes the successful candidate's job title, their position in the organisational structure, the tasks they will do on a day-to-day basis, and other tasks they will need to do less frequently.

Application form
An application form is produced by the business, and it must be completed by everyone applying for a job.

Asking people to complete an application form ensures that the same information is collected from everyone applying for the job.

Curriculum vitae (CV)
A curriculum vitae (CV) is produced by the applicant.

Although there are standard formats for CVs, there is also an element of personal choice: the content and layout of CVs vary from applicant to applicant. This can make it harder for a business to compare candidates.

What information is collected from applicants?

Both application forms and CVs collect similar information, including:

- personal details: name, address, and contact details
- qualifications: GCSEs, A Levels, BTECs, degree, and professional qualifications
- employment history: names of previous employers, as well as brief descriptions of previous job roles and responsibilities
- hobbies: the business wants to get to know the applicant better
- references: names and contact details of individuals who can provide information about the applicant's suitability for the job. This normally includes the applicant's current or most recent employer, and someone who knows the applicant in a personal capacity.

36 Effective recruitment

Recruitment methods

A business can recruit internally and/or externally.

Internal recruitment

Internal recruitment means the successful candidate already works for the business and will be appointed to a new job role within the business. This may be a promotion.

Advantages and disadvantages

Advantages	Disadvantages
✓ Motivates employees who see opportunities for promotion	✗ May demotivate colleagues who apply for the job and do not get promoted
✓ Employer already knows the employee's strengths and weaknesses	✗ The successful candidate cannot bring new ideas and experiences into the business
✓ Employee is already familiar with the business and how it operates	✗ Usually only a small pool of candidates to choose from
✓ Likely to be cheaper and quicker than external recruitment	

External recruitment

External recruitment means the successful candidate is brought into the business from outside.

Advantages and disadvantages

Advantages	Disadvantages
✓ Wider pool of candidates to choose from	✗ Longer and more expensive recruitment process than internal recruitment
✓ Successful candidate can bring new ideas and experiences into the business	✗ May demotivate existing employees who resent someone new being brought into the business
	✗ Successful candidate does not know the business and how it operates

Key terms Make sure you can write a definition for these key terms

curriculum vitae (CV)   external recruitment   internal recruitment
job description   job role   person specification
recruitment process   selection process

Retrieval

Answer the questions below. Cover the answers column with a piece of paper and write down as many answers as you can. Check and repeat.

Questions	Answers
1. State two responsibilities of directors.	Two from: ensuring the business meets its aims and objectives / medium- to long-term decision-making / ensuring the business meets its statutory responsibilities
2. State two responsibilities of senior managers.	The day-to-day running of a business function / managing a group of employees
3. State two responsibilities of supervisors/team leaders.	Two from: overseeing the day-to-day production of goods or services / ensuring quality / responsible for managing a group of employees, usually operational staff
4. What is the difference between operational and support staff?	Office-based staff tend to be called support staff. Factory-based staff tend to be called operational staff
5. What is a person specification?	A recruitment document produced by a business that outlines the qualifications, skills, experience, and characteristics the business is looking for in a successful candidate for a job
6. What is a job description?	A recruitment document produced by a business that outlines the job role and the responsibilities associated with it
7. What is internal recruitment?	The successful candidate already works for the business and will be appointed to a new job role within the business

Previous questions

Use the questions below to check your knowledge from previous chapters.

Questions	Answers
1. What is quality control?	Quality is checked at the end of the production process before the finished product is delivered to customers
2. What is a business's organisational structure?	How employees are organised in terms of who reports to whom
3. What is the difference between a permanent contract and a temporary contract?	With a permanent contract, an employee is contracted to work indefinitely, whereas with a temporary contract, an employee is contracted to work for a set period of time

Practice 36

Exam-style questions

36.1 Which *one* of the following job roles has direct responsibility for operational staff? **(1)**
- **A** Support staff
- **B** Directors
- **C** Supervisors
- **D** Finance managers

36.2 Which two of the following recruitment documents provide information about a job applicant? **(2)**
- **A** Job description
- **B** CV
- **C** Organisational structure
- **D** Application form
- **E** Person specification

36.3 Explain *one* advantage to a business of a hierarchical organisational structure. **(3)**

36.4 Discuss the impact on a business of using internal recruitment. **(6)**

> Sleep Well is a leading manufacturer of beds in the UK. Sleep Well uses quality control in an attempt to ensure 100% customer satisfaction.
>
> The factory employs skilled craftspeople to hand-make the bed frames. Unskilled workers work on production lines where the mattresses are made. Each bed sells for between £1500 and £3000.
>
> At the moment, there are four supervisors and each of them is responsible for two skilled craftspeople and four unskilled workers.
>
> Some of the operational staff have been with the business for over 20 years. Recently, there has been a rise in the number of faulty beds reaching customers, and this is causing costs to rise. Both the finance manager and the operations manager are unhappy. They have asked for a meeting with Archie, the human resources manager, to discuss the problem. Archie has suggested that Sleep Well recruits two new supervisors.

36.5 Define the term 'span of control'. **(1)**

36.6 State *one* job role at Sleep Well. **(1)**

36.7 Analyse the impact of operating quality control at Sleep Well. **(6)**

36.8 Sleep Well wants to recruit two new supervisors to reduce the number of faulty goods reaching customers. It is considering two options:

Option 1: internal recruitment

Option 2: external recruitment.

Justify which *one* of these two options Sleep Well should choose. **(9)**

> **EXAM TIP**
>
> 'Justify' questions require you to decide which option you think is best for the business in the case study. Before you start writing your answers, consider the advantages and disadvantages of both options, and decide which option you think is best. When writing your answer, write one paragraph about the advantage of your chosen option and a second paragraph about a disadvantage of that same option. You have now written a balanced argument by looking at both sides and can finish your answer by adding your conclusion.

Knowledge

37 Effective training and development

How do businesses train and develop employees?

Employees are a valuable asset to a business. Most businesses will, therefore, invest in training and developing employees, providing them with the necessary knowledge and skills to carry out their job roles efficiently.

Well-trained employees can give a business a competitive advantage, ensuring quality products and good customer service, less waste and fewer mistakes.

> **LINK**
> Look back at Chapter 31 to remind yourself about the concept of quality and its importance.

Different ways of training and developing employees

There are a number of different ways to train and develop employees.

Formal training	This is training that follows a structured program of learning, which may lead to a qualification.
	It is normally delivered by a specialist trainer or teacher, and can take place in the workplace or at an educational organisation such as a local college.
Informal training	This is training that is delivered as and when it is needed. It tends not to lead to a qualification.
	It is often delivered by other employees within the workplace.
Self-learning	An employee takes responsibility for improving their knowledge or skills without the support of a structured program of learning.
	This could include watching YouTube videos, listening to podcasts, or reading around a subject.
Ongoing training for all employees	Training should be seen as an ongoing process, not just something offered to new or inexperienced employees. All staff should be given opportunities to learn and develop.
	Many businesses have a commitment to continuing professional development (CPD), to develop and improve.
Target setting and performance reviews	Each employee meets with their manager or a member of the human resources team for a performance review. Performance reviews usually take place annually.
	During the meeting, the employee's progress is discussed; their strengths and achievements, as well as areas for improvement, are identified; and training needs are established.
	The performance review will be used to set targets, and the employee's progress towards the targets will be measured on a regular basis or at the next performance review.

Training employees: motivation and retention

There is a link between training, and motivation and **retention**. Motivation is the desire to succeed. Retention is the amount of time an employee stays working for a business.

- Training and developing employees makes them feel valued, because they appreciate that the business is investing in them.
  ↓
- Employees who feel valued are happier and more motivated, leading to a better working environment and less time off.
  ↓
- As a result, employees are less likely to leave the business and take their knowledge and skills elsewhere.
  ↓
- In turn, higher retention means a more experienced workforce and lower recruitment costs.

REMEMBER

The positive relationship between training, and motivation and retention is clear, but there are potential disadvantages of training for a business. For example, a business can invest in training an employee, only for the employee to use the new skills and experience they have gained to get a job with a competitor.

Training employees: new technology

As technology advances, businesses may need to retrain employees who need to learn new skills or develop existing skills. For example, they may need to:

- learn how to operate new machinery
- learn how to use new software packages
- learn how to use more advanced features within existing software packages
- develop their technical skills to enable them to work remotely.

Key terms — Make sure you can write a definition for this key term: retention

Retrieval

Answer the questions below. Cover the answers column with a piece of paper and write down as many answers as you can. Check and repeat.

Questions | Answers

#	Questions	Answers
1	What is training?	Providing employees with the necessary knowledge and skills to carry out their job roles efficiently
2	What is the difference between formal training and informal training?	Formal training is training that follows a structured program of learning, which may lead to a qualification. Informal training is training that is delivered as and when it is needed; it tends not to lead to a qualification
3	What is self-learning?	An employee takes responsibility for improving their knowledge or skills without the support of a structured program of learning
4	What is a performance review?	When an employee meets with their manager or a member of the human resources team to discuss their progress
5	Performance reviews are used to set what for employees?	Targets
6	Give two reasons why businesses train and develop employees.	Two from: motivation / retention / to use new technology
7	What does the term 'retention' mean?	The amount of time an employee stays working for a business
8	Employees who feel valued are happier and feel what?	More motivated
9	What does higher retention mean for a business?	A more experienced workforce and lower recruitment costs
10	As technology advances, businesses may need to retrain employees. Why?	Because they need to learn new skills or develop existing skills

Previous questions

Use the questions below to check your knowledge from previous chapters.

#	Questions	Answers
1	State two ways that technology has impacted on ways of working.	It has increased efficiency; it has enabled remote working
2	What is a job description?	A recruitment document produced by a business that outlines the job role and the responsibilities associated with it
3	What is internal recruitment?	The successful candidate already works for the business and will be appointed to a new job role within the business

37 Effective training and development

Practice 37

Exam-style questions

37.1 Which *one* of the following is a reason why businesses train employees? **(1)**

- A Job description
- B Motivation
- C Formal training
- D Reduce retention

37.2 Which *two* of the following are ways of training and developing employees? **(2)**

- A External recruitment
- B Retention rates
- C Self-learning
- D Performance reviews
- E New technology

37.3 Explain *one* benefit to a business of training employees. **(3)**

37.4 Discuss the impact on a business of offering employees flexible hours. **(6)**

> Yorkshire Dental Practices Ltd is a chain of dentists operating in the north of England. Over the last five years, the business has grown from one dental practice to 25 through a series of takeovers. Dental practices are traditionally partnerships with two to six partners, but Yorkshire Dental Practices Ltd saw an opportunity to cut costs and improve customer service by bringing smaller practices together to form one company.
>
> Harvey, the managing director, is keen for customer service to be consistent across all 25 practices. He wants all reception staff to be trained to use the new digital booking system that will be introduced across all 25 practices.
>
> Harvey is also keen for the dental procedures to be consistent across all 25 practices. All of the dental nurses will have a performance review with the most senior dentist at the practice where they work. Targets will be set, which will be reviewed by the senior dentist and the human resources manager every six months.

37.5 Define the term 'partnership'. **(1)**

37.6 Outline *one* training method that Yorkshire Dental Practices Ltd could use to train its reception staff. **(2)**

37.7 Outline *one* reason why Yorkshire Dental Practices Ltd may need to train its reception staff to use new technology. **(2)**

37.8 Analyse the benefit to Yorkshire Dental Practices Ltd of training and developing all its employees. **(6)**

37.9 Analyse the advantages to Yorkshire Dental Practices Ltd of inorganic growth. **(6)**

> **EXAM TIP**
>
> When answering 'Analyse' questions, you need to develop each point that you make using phrases like 'because', 'therefore' and 'this means that'. You can either make one relevant point followed by five development points, or you can make one relevant point followed by two development points plus one development point followed by three development points, but you need at least five development points.

Knowledge

38 Motivation

The importance of motivation in the workplace

Motivation is the desire to succeed, and motivated employees can give a business a competitive advantage. A motivated workplace can help a business attract employees, retain employees, and increase productivity.

Attracting employees

If a business has a reputation as a good employer, it is easier to attract new employees and the best talent.

People are more likely to apply for a job if they believe the business will invest in training and development, pay them well, and provide good working conditions.

Retaining employees

Motivated employees are more likely to work for a business for a longer period of time than people who don't like their jobs.

This makes it easier for a business to provide consistent levels of customer service and to meet demand, because it does not have to deal with staff shortages. This, in turn, leads to lower recruitment costs.

Productivity

Productivity is the output per unit of input, and labour productivity is how much an employee can produce. Employees who have worked for a business for a long time are familiar with their job roles and more skilled, leading to higher labour productivity.

This results in lower costs, an ability to match supply to demand, less waste, and greater customer satisfaction.

> **REVISION TIP**
>
> In Chapter 37, you learned about the relationship between training, and motivation and retention. When revising motivation, consider how training helps attract employees, retain employees, and increase productivity.

Key terms — Make sure you can write a definition for these key terms

job enrichment   job rotation

How do businesses motivate employees?

Businesses use financial and non-financial methods to motivate employees. Financial methods involve a monetary reward, whereas non-financial methods focus on the day-to-day working practices of employees.

Financial methods of motivating employees

Remuneration
Remuneration refers to the payment received for work done, and businesses can motivate employees by paying them more.

Bonus
A bonus is an additional payment paid for meeting a target, and businesses can motivate employees to meet their targets by paying them a bonus if they do.

Commission
Commission is an additional payment paid for each sale made, and businesses can motivate their employees to sell their products by paying them commission on each sale.

Promotion
A promotion is a new job in a higher level of the organisational structure, which often comes with more responsibility and higher remuneration. Businesses can motivate employees by providing them with a route to promotion.

Fringe benefits
Fringe benefits are benefits with a monetary value that a business gives to its employees in addition to the remuneration they receive. Receiving health care, a company car, or a gym membership as a perk of the job can be very motivating for employees.

Non-financial methods of motivating employees

Job rotation
Job rotation means performing a wider variety of tasks at the same level. For example, switching from stacking shelves during one shift at a supermarket to operating a till on the next shift. Mixing things up like this can be very motivating for employees, because it helps to prevent boredom.

Job enrichment
Job enrichment means performing a wider variety of tasks with varying levels of responsibility. For example, operating a till at a supermarket and cashing up at the end of a shift. This is a way to develop employees and prepare them for future promotion, which can be very motivating.

Autonomy
Being given a greater degree of independence to decide exactly how to perform tasks can motivate employees, and it is a good way of developing employees too.

Retrieval

Answer the questions below. Cover the answers column with a piece of paper and write down as many answers as you can. Check and repeat.

#	Questions	Answers
1	What is motivation?	The desire to succeed
2	A motivated workplace can help a business do what?	Attract employees, retain employees, and increase productivity
3	Motivated employees are more likely to do what than people who don't like their jobs?	Work for a business for a longer period of time
4	What does higher labour productivity result in?	Lower costs, an ability to match supply to demand, less waste, and greater customer satisfaction
5	What do financial methods to motivate employees involve?	A monetary reward
6	What do non-financial methods of motivating employees focus on?	The day-to-day working practices of employees
7	Name three financial methods of motivating employees.	Three from: remuneration / bonus / commission / promotion / fringe benefits
8	What is an additional payment paid for meeting a target called?	Bonus
9	Which financial method of motivation involves an additional payment paid for each sale made?	Commission
10	Name three non-financial methods of motivating employees.	Job rotation; job enrichment; autonomy
11	What is job rotation?	Performing a wider variety of tasks at the same level
12	What is job enrichment?	Performing a wider variety of tasks with varying levels of responsibility

Previous questions

Use the questions below to check your knowledge from previous chapters.

#	Questions	Answers
1	What is the difference between operational and support staff?	Office-based staff tend to be called support staff. Factory-based staff tend to be called operational staff
2	Give two reasons why businesses train and develop employees.	Two from: motivation/retention/to use new technology
3	Employees who feel valued are happier and feel what?	More motivated

Practice 38

Exam-style questions

38.1 Which *one* of the following is a benefit of motivating employees in the workplace? **(1)**

- **A** Lower retention rates
- **B** Easier to attract employees
- **C** Remuneration
- **D** Job enrichment

38.2 Which *two* of the following are non-financial methods of motivating employees? **(2)**

- **A** Fringe benefits
- **B** Job rotation
- **C** Autonomy
- **D** Remuneration
- **E** Promotion

38.3 Explain *one* reason why motivation in the workplace is important to a business. **(3)**

38.4 Discuss the impact on a business of using non-financial methods of motivation. **(6)**

> Bakers is a national chain of car showrooms selling used cars and small vans. Each showroom has a receptionist, an office manager, a finance assistant, a showroom manager and three to eight sales assistants. The showroom managers are responsible for keeping the website up to date with the cars for sale, conducting performance reviews for the sales assistants, and reporting weekly sales figures to the head office in Bedford.
>
> The sales assistants all receive a basic salary of £26,000 per year, and 5% commission on each sale. Head office sets each showroom a monthly sales target. If met, all employees at the showroom receive a £250 bonus. Some of the sales assistants feel this is unfair: they are making the sales so they should receive the bonus. As a result, there has been a rise in the number of sales assistants leaving Bakers.

38.5 Define the term 'bonus'. **(1)**

38.6 State *one* financial method used to motivate the sales assistants. **(1)**

EXAM TIP
You do not need to write complete sentences to answer 'State' questions. You can use just one or two words and save the time to plan your longer answers.

38.7 Outline *one* benefit to Bakers of using performance reviews. **(2)**

38.8 Analyse the impact on Bakers of using financial methods to motivate employees. **(6)**

38.9 In order to improve staff retention, Bakers is considering two options:

Option 1: increase the commission paid on each sale to 7.5%

Option 2: add a new layer to the organisational structure so that each showroom has a sales manager.

Justify which *one* of these two options Bakers should choose. **(9)**

Exam-style questions

Lido Leisure plc is the UK's largest chain of outdoor swimming pools. It owns 56 premises across the country, each with a swimming pool, a gym, a fitness studio, a spa and a cafe. It has many employees on a range of contracts, including full-time, part-time, and flexible-hours contracts.

Number of employees on 1 January 2023	2240
Number of employees that left in 2023	120
Number of employees recruited in 2023	360

▲ **Table 1** Number of employees at Lido Leisure plc, 2023

Due to the nature of the work, it is important that employees have appropriate qualifications. Lifeguards need to be excellent swimmers and have a National Pool Lifeguard Qualification (NPLQ), while gym instructors must have at least a Level 3 NVQ Diploma in Personal Training. The business has an apprentice scheme where it formally trains a number of junior employees, with senior employees providing additional informal training to develop skills. This enables Lido Leisure plc to have a fairly flat, decentralised organisational structure. Employees have a high degree of autonomy when delivering classes, such as dance, cycling and yoga.

Some elements of working at a Lido can be boring. To reduce the boredom, Lido Leisure plc uses job rotation: for example, employees with the appropriate qualifications rotate between lifeguarding and working in the gym. Job enrichment is also used: employees can develop their own workouts for customers, or use their own music playlists for aqua aerobics. The company also uses a range of financial methods to motivate employees, including paying more than competitors, and providing fringe benefits that include free use of the facilities.

38.10 State *one* type of contract that employees at Lido Leisure plc might be offered. **(1)**

38.11 Using the information in Table 1, calculate to two decimal places the percentage increase in the number of employees at Lido Leisure plc between 1 January 2023 and 31 December 2023. You are advised to show your workings. **(2)**

> **EXAM TIP**
> When answering 'Calculate' questions, always show your workings in the space provided on the exam paper.

38.12 Outline *one* drawback of informal training for Lido Leisure plc. **(2)**

38.13 Analyse the impact on Lido Leisure plc of having a decentralised organisational structure. **(6)**

38.14 To ensure Lido Leisure plc has sufficient employees to meet customer needs, it is considering two options:

Option 1: internal recruitment

Option 2: external recruitment.

Justify which *one* of these two options Lido Leisure plc should choose. **(9)**

38.15 Evaluate the importance of financial methods of motivation to help Lido Leisure plc to retain its workforce. You should use the information provided as well as your knowledge of business. **(12)**

> **EXAM TIP**
> 'Evaluate' questions require you to consider both sides of the argument. To answer this question, you should discuss the importance of financial methods of motivation, followed by a discussion about why financial methods of motivation may not be enough and why non-financial methods of motivation may be better.

OXFORD
UNIVERSITY PRESS

Great Clarendon Street, Oxford, OX2 6DP, United Kingdom

Oxford University Press is a department of the University of Oxford.
It furthers the University's objective of excellence in research, scholarship,
and education by publishing worldwide. Oxford is a registered trade mark
of Oxford University Press in the UK and in certain other countries.

© Oxford University Press 2025

Written by Helen Coupland-Smith and Stefan Wytwyckyj
The moral rights of the authors have been asserted

First published in 2025

All rights reserved. No part of this publication may be reproduced, stored
in a retrieval system, transmitted, used for text and data mining, or used
for training artificial intelligence, in any form or by any means, without
the prior permission in writing of Oxford University Press, or as expressly
permitted by law, by licence or under terms agreed with the appropriate
reprographics rights organization. Enquiries concerning reproduction
outside the scope of the above should be sent to the Rights Department,
Oxford University Press, at the address above.

You must not circulate this work in any other form and you must impose
this same condition on any acquirer

British Library Cataloguing in Publication Data
Data available

978-1-38-206772-0
978-1-38-206771-3 (ebook)

10 9 8 7 6 5 4 3 2 1

The manufacturing process conforms to the environmental regulations
of the country of origin.

Printed in China by Shanghai Offset Printing Products Ltd.

The manufacturer's authorised representative in the EU for product
safety is Oxford University Press España S.A. of El Parque Empresarial
San Fernando de Henares, Avenida de Castilla, 2 – 28830 Madrid
(www.oup.es/en or product.safety@oup.com). OUP España S.A. also
acts as importer into Spain of products made by the manufacturer.

Acknowledgements

The publisher would like to thank Antonitsa Camacho Owusu-Opoku
and Adam Robbins for sharing their expertise and feedback in the
development of this resource.

The publisher would like to thank the following for permissions to use
copyright material:

Photos: p12: 4045 / Shutterstock; **p26**: David JC / Shutterstock; **p46**: Shutterstock AI Generator / Shutterstock; **p64**: G Estudios Multimedia / Shutterstock; **p84**: marc macdonald / Alamy Stock Photo; **p104**: parkerphotography / Alamy Stock Photo; **p120**: New Africa / Shutterstock; **p122**(l): Cavan Images / Alamy Stock Photo; **p122**(m): ManWithaCamera Melbourne / Alamy Stock Photo; **p122**(r): Michele D'Ottavio / Alamy Stock Photo; **p134**: f.t.Photographer / Shutterstock; **p146**: Adam Yee / Shutterstock; **p168**: Clare McEwen / Shutterstock

Artwork by Q2A Media

Although we have made every effort to trace and contact all copyright
holders before publication this has not been possible in all cases.
If notified, the publisher will rectify any errors or omissions at the
earliest opportunity.

Links to third party websites are provided by Oxford in good faith
and for information only. Oxford disclaims any responsibility for the
materials contained in any third party website referenced in this work.